THE
PSYCHOTHERAPIST-PATIENT PRIVILEGE
A CRITICAL EXAMINATION

Publication Number 1070

AMERICAN LECTURE SERIES

A Monograph in

The BANNERSTONE DIVISION of
AMERICAN SERIES IN BEHAVIORAL SCIENCE AND LAW

Edited by

RALPH SLOVENKO, B.E., LL.B., M.A., Ph.D.
Professor of Law and Psychiatry
Wayne State University Law School
Detroit, Michigan

The Authors

Daniel W. Shuman, *Professor of Law, Southern Methodist University School of Law, Dallas, Texas; B.S. 1969, J.D. 1972, University of Arizona*

Myron F. Weiner, *Professor and Vice Chairman, Department of Psychiatry, University of Texas Health Science Center at Dallas, Texas; M.D. 1957, Tulane University*

THE PSYCHOTHERAPIST-PATIENT PRIVILEGE

A Critical Examination

By

DANIEL W. SHUMAN

and

MYRON F. WEINER

With a Foreword by

RALPH SLOVENKO, B.E., LL.B., M.A., Ph.D.

Professor of Law and Psychiatry
Wayne State University Law School
Detroit, Michigan

CHARLES C THOMAS • PUBLISHER
Springfield • Illinois • U.S.A.

Published and Distributed Throughout the World by

CHARLES C THOMAS • PUBLISHER
2600 South First Street
Springfield, Illinois 62794-9265

ISBN 0-398-05338-3

Library of Congress Catalog Card Number: 87-1962

With THOMAS BOOKS *careful attention is given to all details of manufacturing and design. It is the Publisher's desire to present books that are satisfactory as to their physical qualities and artistic possibilities and appropriate for their particular use.* THOMAS BOOKS *will be true to those laws of quality that assure a good name and good will.*

Printed in the United States of America
SC-R-3

Library of Congress Cataloging-in-Publication Data

Shuman, Daniel W.
The psychotherapist-patient privilege.

(American lecture series ; publication no. 1070)
"A monograph in the Bannerstone Division of American series in behavioral science and law"—P. facing t.p.
Includes bibliographies and index.
"SC-R-3"—T.p. verso.
1. Confidential communications—Physicians—United States. 2. Psychotherapists—Legal status, laws, etc.—United States. I. Weiner, Myron F., 1934– II. Title. III. Series. [DNLM: 1. Confidentiality. 2. Physician-Patient Relations. 3. Psychotherapy. W 740 S562p]
KF8959.P4S52 1987 347.73'66 87-1962
ISBN 0-398-05338-3 347.30766

This book is dedicated . . .
. . . to our parents

FOREWORD

Classic theory holds that testimonial privilege—or shield law—protecting confidentiality is essential to the practice of psychotherapy. Is a shield really essential? Is believing in a shield as good as having one? There is a considerable body of thought that a shield protecting the confidentiality of communications is crucial to psychotherapy and that without it, treatment would be impeded. Perhaps the most quoted statement about the psychotherapist-patient relationship is from the Group for the Advancement of Psychiatry, which stated in 1960:

> Among physicians, the psychiatrist has a special need to maintain confidentiality. His capacity to help his patients is completely dependent upon their willingness and ability to talk freely. This makes it difficult if not impossible for him to function without being able to assure his patients of confidentiality and, indeed, privileged communication. Where there may be exceptions to this general rule . . . , there is wide agreement that confidentiality is a *sine qua non* for successful psychiatric treatment. The relationship may well be likened to that of the priest-penitent or the lawyer-client. Psychiatrists not only explore the very depths of their patients' conscious, but their unconscious feelings and attitudes as well. Therapeutic effectiveness necessitates going beyond a patient's awareness and, in order to do this, it must be possible to communicate freely. A threat to secrecy blocks successful treatment.

The story behind this book: When doing an article on evidentiary issues in civil commitment proceedings, Professor Daniel W. Shuman pondered about the empirical support for a psychotherapist-patient privilege. The more he thought about it, the more it concerned him that society was being asked to accept as an article of faith something that ought to be clarified by empirical research. His work with Dr. Myron F. Weiner began as an effort to discover that research and, not finding any, they began their studies. They undertook empirical investigation in the United States and Canada, and in the course of those studies they became curious about the historical and ethical aspects of the privilege which led to their research on those topics.

In the course of their research, the authors came full circle. Initially, they were taken in by the armchair empirical arguments for the privilege. Their empirical research, however, convinced them that these arguments lacked good evidence. Ultimately, their thinking evolved to a deontological point of view. Their conclusion now is that privilege is important, not for the reasons initially advocated, but for reasons that suggest a very different way of looking at and articulating privilege. They would recommend balancing privilege in the context of individual cases rather than articulating a set rule and exceptions.

Today, about 45 states of the United States have some form of privilege statute for psychotherapy. None of them is absolute. Either through judicial interpretation or statutory exception, communications when relevant and material to an issue in litigation are placed outside of it. The usual exceptions include civil commitment proceedings, child abuse and neglect cases, court-ordered examinations, and situations where the patient as litigant uses his mental condition as part of the underlying claim or defense. It takes a stretch of imagination to envision a case calling for testimony of a therapist that would not fall under the exceptions. Judges do not uniformly interpret the scope of the privilege or the exceptions. The balancing that takes place varies widely. Some judges are hostile to the very notion of privilege and, as a consequence, they interpret the exceptions broadly. Others, on the other hand, restrict the exceptions.

Justice Matthew Tobriner of the California Supreme Court observed in the much publicized decision in 1970 compelling Dr. Joseph Lifschutz to testify: "Although petitioner has submitted affidavits of psychotherapists who concur in his assertion that total confidentiality is essential to the practice of their profession, we cannot blind ourselves to the fact that the practice of psychotherapy has grown, indeed flourished, in an environment of non-absolute privilege.... Whether psychotherapy's development has progressed only because patients are ignorant of the existing legal environment can only be a matter for speculation; psychotherapists certainly have been aware of the limitations of their recognized privilege for sometime."

In the course of this study, most individuals interviewed by the authors were not aware if a privilege did exist, and when questioned, they indicated that the existence or lack thereof would not affect their decision to seek therapy. When the members of the sample group were told to assume that no privilege existed, they indicated a lesser willingness to disclose. However, the authors conclude that disclosure by clients would probably not be greatly enhanced by a statutory privilege. The basic reason, they say, why patients hesitate to talk about something or other is because they fear the judgment of their therapist.

This pioneering book is the joint effort of a law professor and psychiatrist, who have done distinguished work. Professor Shuman is a member of the law faculty of Southern Methodist University and at one time visiting scholar at McGill University, and Assistant Attorney General and Chief Counsel for Behavioral Health and Health Care Institution Licensing and Regulation in Arizona. Dr. Weiner is Professor of Clinical Psychiatry and Vice Chairman, Department of Psychiatry, University of Texas Health Science Center at Dallas. They combine in this book the learning of law and psychiatry.

RALPH SLOVENKO
Professor of Law and Psychiatry
Wayne State University

PREFACE

This book is the product of a six-year collaboration between a professor of law and a professor of psychiatry, both of whom are concerned about practical matters of judicial factfinding and the conduct of psychotherapy.

Our work began with the senior author's research into the rules of evidence in civil commitment proceedings, in which he noted the wide acceptance of support for a therapist-patient privilege based on the contention that confidentiality is a sine qua non of effective psychotherapy. Assuming that such a widely held belief must have an empirical basis, he sought the empirical evidence. After finding little empirical evidence to substantiate the need for privilege, he turned to the second author for assistance in a detailed inquiry into the psychiatric literature. Here, too, the objective findings were sparse, but the sentiment in favor of privilege was strong.

The authors concluded that the data uncovered in their study of legal and psychiatric literature was inadequate to substantiate empirically either a need or a lack of need for privilege. At about the same time, however, an opportunity was presented to study the effects of a recently enacted psychotherapist-patient privilege statute in the state of Texas. Other studies followed, including a study of the two states in which no form of therapist-patient privilege existed, and a study in another country contrasting a region in which a professional secret exists with one in which there is no comparable barrier to disclosure.

These studies are balanced by a review of the historical origins of privilege within the healing professions and within the legal profession.

It is the authors' hope that their exploration in depth of one aspect of the therapist-patient relationship will add the missing element of objectivity to the controversy surrounding privilege.

Daniel W. Shuman, J.D.
Myron F. Weiner, M.D.
Dallas, Texas

ACKNOWLEDGMENTS

This book is the culmination of numerous studies in different disciplines and different locations over a six year time period. Some of these studies have been published separately and some will appear for the first time in this book. The research for these studies has been generously supported by the Southern Methodist University School of Law and the Department of Psychiatry of the University of Texas Health Science Center at Dallas. This support has come in the form of research grants as well as advice and encouragement from our respective deans, department chairs, and colleagues.

Over the years many students have worked as research assistants on the studies that have led up to this book. Maureen Armour, Meg Davidson, Cathy Farlow, Rande Herrell, and Andrew Ragusin are all now successful attorneys without whose labors as student research assistants this book would not have been possible.

Nicola Stout, Carolyn Magers, and Gary Satoe at the law school and Lisa Jackson and Carol Laebs at the medical school turned our drafts into a polished manuscript that, if nothing else, looked like a book.

To all of these individuals and organizations we wish to express our sincere appreciation.

CONTENTS

THE PSYCHOTHERAPIST-PATIENT PRIVILEGE
A CRITICAL EXAMINATION

Chapter 1

INTRODUCTION

The importance of confidentiality in therapy for persons seeking help for mental or emotional problems seems, at first blush, almost too obvious to require explanation. The prospect of a therapist treating mental or emotional disorders disclosing in a nontherapeutic context the intimate details of a patient's life revealed in therapy, without the patient's consent, threatens to undermine the therapeutic relationship and raises a broad spectrum of concerns about privacy. It is not at all surprising that the professional codes of ethics of the American Psychiatric Association and the American Psychological Association require that these professionals respect the confidences of their patients.[1]

The judicial system, generally operating in a sphere independent of psychotherapist-patient relations, reaches decisions on questions that affect the life, liberty, and property of litigants. It would appear obvious, without the need for extensive support, that, to the extent that these judicial decisions turn on factual determinations, they should be as accurate as possible. Because the accuracy of these judicial determinations depends, in part, on the availability of evidence to the decisionmaker, access to all relevant evidence is important to the judicial system.[2]

Both efficacious psychotherapy and accurate judicial decision making are strongly supported in our society. Mental or emotional problems of varying degrees are pervasive in our society.[3] In addition to serious mental illness requiring hospitalization and/or drug treatment, emotional problems stemming from marital difficulties, losing a loved one through death or divorce, loss of employment, or a parent-child conflict, touch virtually every family at some time. Our society has supported therapy for these problems in a multitude of fashions. For example, we provide public insurance coverage for the treatment of mental or emotional disorders through tax dollars and support private insurance coverage of these disorders through beneficial tax treatments. In addition, we license health care professionals in an effort to ensure high quality care.

Accurate judicial decisionmaking also occupies a high societal priority.

We rely on the courts to interpret and apply laws affecting virtually every facet of our lives. If the members of society lack confidence in the correctness of judicial decisions on these laws, the legal fabric of our society is threatened.

In most instances, these two systems operate in parallel fashion, neither disturbing or conflicting with the other. However, in some instances these systems come into conflict. For example, a married couple in the throes of a divorce disputes the custody of their two young children. The mother informs her attorney that the father has expressed sexual feelings about one of the children, for which he is currently participating in individual psychotherapy. Should the father's therapist be compelled to disclose the confidences of the father relative to the likelihood that he may sexually molest the children if granted custody. Is it appropriate for society in this circumstance to intrude on the confidentiality of this relationship? Will compelled disclosure dissuade this father and others like him from seeking help for these problems? Will failure to require disclosure of this information substantially increase the risk of an erroneous judicial decision on the question of custody, thereby placing the children at risk?

Another example involves a woman who has been in psychotherapy for the past year and a half is charged with murdering the married man with whom she had been having an affair for the past two years. She raises the insanity defense but does not call the therapist who has been treating her. Should the prosecution be permitted to call this therapist as a witness and compel the therapist to disclose confidential information that might bear on the defendant's mental status at the time of the offense? Is a judicial decision made without this information likely to be substantially less accurate than a judicial decision made with this information, thus increasing the risk of an erroneous judicial decision? Will compelled disclosure of this information dissuade persons with violent tendencies that might be effectively addressed in therapy from seeking therapy?

These are but two examples of the kinds of conflicts that arise between confidentiality in psychotherapy and accuracy in judicial decision making. Confidentiality as mandated by professional ethics limits gratuitous disclosures by the therapist but provides no limitation on judicial compulsion to disclose. The decision to recognize a right of the patient in psychotherapy to prevent the court from compelling the therapist's testimony is a relational privilege—physician-patient, psychiatrist-patient, psychologist-patient, or psychotherapist-patient. Although the criteria for deciding whether to recognize one of these privileges in a jurisdiction are often not articulated, they tend to be either utilitarian or deontological.

The utilitarian approach to privilege argues that privilege, particularly in the context of treatment for mental or emotional problems, is necessary for effective therapy. Because of the extremely sensitive problems discussed in psychotherapy and the stigma attached to being a patient for these problems, prospective patients will not consider psychotherapy in the absence of the limitation on disclosure created by a privilege. Even if prospective patients do consider therapy, the utilitarian argument maintains, they will not be candid with their therapist or trust their therapist, both of which are necessary for effective therapy. Support for these arguments has largely been based on anecdotal evidence. This book has its origins in the authors' attempt to discover empirical research to support these theories and, subsequently, the authors' own empirical studies. Chapter 3 explores these theoretical justifications in detail and Chapter 5 describes the research on this question conducted by the authors and others. The implications of this research are analyzed in Chapter 6.

The deontological approach to privilege argues that privilege is important, not because relationships will falter in the absence of privilege, but because it is inappropriate for society to intrude in this private sphere. Thus, the deontological argument favoring privilege is unconcerned with whether patients will be effectively treated should a psychotherapist-patient privilege not exist. Instead, it is concerned that privilege should exist to keep the government out of patient-therapist communications. This argument has not been used frequently to justify a psychotherapist or other related privileges in common law jurisdictions and its precepts and consequences have, therefore, not been carefully explored in common law jurisdictions. Chapters 4 and 6 address, in part, the deontological arguments for and consequences of recognizing a psychotherapist-patient privilege.

Frequently, both the utilitarian and deontological arguments for privilege invoke the proscriptions on breaching the confidentiality of therapist-patient communications found in the therapist's ethical codes. Chapter 2 traces the development of these codes and their treatment of confidentiality as a justification for the recognition of a privilege.

The issues raised in the decision whether to recognize a privilege have been addressed in legal systems other than our own. Chapter 4 traces the historical roots of privilege in common and civil law legal systems and the manner in which these systems have come to grips with the competing tensions.

Based upon the historical, theoretical, and empirical research described in Chapters 2–5, a new approach to privilege is proposed in Chapter 6. This new approach is more responsive to the way in which privilege is addressed in practice and provides a more flexible, careful method of accomodating the conflicting values at issue.

Throughout this book, when the term psychotherapist is used, it is intended to include physicians specializing in the practice of psychiatry and clinical psychologists.[4] This is not intended to slight the role of others, such as psychiatric social workers in the delivery of mental health care or the arguments in favor of extending a privilege to these professions.[5] Rather, this limitation is a convenient place to draw the line for discussion and corresponds to legislative line-drawing in this field.

This book is the result of a critical reexamination of the way in which we in the United States think about privilege in the context of psychotherapist-patient relationships. It is not intended to be a treatise on the existing law. Yet, to understand how we think about the psychotherapist-patient privilege it is of no minor importance what the law is now. It is from that perspective this, the following summary of United States law on the psychotherapist-patient privilege, is presented.

American courts adopted the approach of English courts in refusing to recognize a common law basis for a physician-patient privilege.[6] However, beginning in New York in 1828 and continuing through the present, state legislatures have created statutory privileges.[7] As of this date every state but South Carolina and West Virginia has enacted either a physician, psychiatrist, psychologist, or psychotherapist-patient privilege.[8] In many jurisdictions, either in addition to or in lieu of a physician patient-privilege, psychiatrist, psychologist and psychotherapist-patient privileges exist. The basic requirements for all these privileges are similar. These privileges protect against compelled judicial disclosure of confidential communications between a person seeking treatment and a therapist, as defined in the relevant statute.[9] In the case of physician-patient privilege statutes, a physician is usually defined to include allopathic and osteopathic physicians but not chiropractors, pharmacists, dentists, or nurses.[10] Psychologist-patient privileges define psychologist as one licensed to practice psychology.[11] In some states a further restriction is made including only clinical psychologists within the privileges's purview.[12] Psychiatrist-patient privileges apply to physicians who specialize in the practice of psychiatry or devote a substantial portion of their practice to psychiatry.[13] Psychotherapist-patient privileges typically include both psychiatrists and psychologists within the definition of psychotherapist.[14]

The limitation of these privileges to confidential communications relevant to treatment excludes communications made in the presence of nonessential third parties[15] or on a subject unrelated to treatment.[16] Thus, an examination made under the authority of a court order that entails a requirement of a report to the court and counsel is not privileged both because it contemplates a public disclosure of the communications and because it is directed towards testimony and not treatment.[17]

The protection of the privilege continues after the death of the patient.[18] It may, however, be waived by the patient. An express waiver of privilege may occur in an application for insurance.[19] An implied waiver, conduct inconsistent with a desire to maintain confidentiality, is illustrated by calling the physician as a witness and asking questions about the communication[20] or filing a lawsuit concerning the condition for which treatment was received.[21]

In addition, exceptions to the privilege are recognized in every state. Not every state recognizes the same exceptions and some recognize more than others, but all recognize some. The category of cases to which an exception applies includes child abuse or custody,[22] criminal,[23] civil commitment,[24] and worker's compensation.[25]

Generally, the only difference in the application of the physician, psychiatrist, psychologist, and psychotherapist-patient privilege is the definition of the therapist. However, there are two issues that raise special problems in the case of the psychiatrist, psychologist, and psychotherapist-patient privileges—disclosure of the patient's identity and group therapy. The effect of a privilege is normally to protect against the disclosure of the confidential communication, not the identity of the patient.[26] Although forceful arguments have been made to distinguish the case of patients in psychotherapy from general medical problems, this argument has not usually been successful.[27]

Group therapy, a method of treatment unique to psychotherapy, involves the presence of persons other than the therapist and the patient between whom the communication sought to be protected occurs. Although some limited acceptance exists for cloaking communications made in group therapy under a privilege,[28] the statutory language of the privilege and the practical consequences of controlling the disclosures of the other members of the group generally combine to defeat its effect in this context.[29]

FOOTNOTES, CHAPTER 1

1. American Psychiatric Association, *The Principles of Medical Ethics, with Annotations Especially Applicable to Psychiatry,* 130 Am. J. Psychiatry 1058 (1973); 246 J.A.M.A. 2187 (1981); American Psychological Association, *Ethical Standards of Psychologist,* 36 Am. Psychol. 633 (1981).
2. J. Thayer, A Preliminary Treatise on Evidence at the Common Law 530 (1898).
3. U.S. Dept. of H.E. W., The Alcohol, Drug Abuse, and Mental Health National Data Book (1980).
4. *See* Proposed Fed. R. Evid. 504(a)(2):

   > A "psychotherapist" is (A) a person authorized to practice medicine in any state or any nation or reasonably believed by the patient to be so, while engaged in the diagnosis or treatment of a mental or emotional condition, including drug addiction, or (B) a person licensed or certified as a psychologist under the laws of any state or nation, while similarly engaged.

5. *See* Comment, *Underprivileged Communications: Extension of the Psychotherapist-Patient Privilege to Patients of Psychiatric Social Workers,* 61 Cal. L. Rev. 1050 (1973); Note, *The Social Worker Client Relationship and Privileged Communications,* 1965 Wash. U. L. Q. 362.
6. Whalen v. Roe, 429 U.S. 589, 602 n. 28 (1977); Duchess of Kingston's Case, 20 How. St. Trials 355, 573 (1776). One state has recognized a common law basis for the privilege (Allred v. State, 554 P.2d 411 (Alaska 1976)) and some support has been found for a constitutionally based privilege relying on Griswold v. Connecticut, 381 U.S. 479 (1965) and Roe v. Wade, 410 U.S. 113 (1973). See Shuman, Psychiatric and Psychological Evidence § 10.09 (1986).
7. For an historical discussion of this subject see Chapter 4.
8. Shuman and Weiner *The Privilege Study: An Empirical Examination of the psychotherapist-Patient privilege.* 60 N.C. L. Rev. 893, 907 n. 100 (1982).
9. J. Weinstein & M. Berger, Weinstein's Evidence § 504[01] at 504-09 (1982).
10. E. Cleary, McCormick on Evidence §§ 99, at 246 n. 1 (3rd ed. 1984).
11. Ariz. Rev. Stat. Ann. § 32-2085 (Supp. 1986).
12. Conn. Gen. Stat. Ann. § 52-146(c)(a) (West Supp. 1983).
13. Ala. Code § 34-36-2 (Supp. 1984); Conn. Gen. Stat. § 52-146d (1983).
14. Fla. Stat. Ann. § 90.503 (West 1979); N.M. R. Evid. 504 (1978); Tex. R. Evid. 510.
15. A more functional approach to this question has taken place recently. Thus while any third person was once thought to destroy confidentiality, the current focus is the functional necessity of the third party's presence. Rudnick v. Superior Court, 11 Cal. 3d 924, 523 P.2d 643, 114 Cal Rptr. 603 (1974) (nurse

assisting physician); Grosslight v. Superior Court, 72 Cal. App. 3d 502, 140 Cal. Rptr. 278 (1977) (communication by patient's family to therapists).

16. San Francisco v. Superior Court, 37 Cal. 2d 227, 231 P.2d 26 (1951).
17. State v. Cole, 295 N.W.2d 29 (Iowa 1980); Jones v. State, 610 N.W.2d 535 (Tex. Civ. App. 1980), writ ref'd n.r.e.
18. Bassil v. Ford Motor Co., 278 Mich. 173, 270 N.W. 258 (1936).
19. United States v. Radetsky, 535 F.2d 556, 569 n. 14 (10th Cir. 1976), cert. denied 429 U.S. 820 (1976).
20. State v. Carter, 641 S.W.2d 54 (Mo. 1982); People v. Smith, 59 N.Y.2d 156, 451 N.E.2d 157, 464 N.Y.S.2d 399 (1983).
21. San Francisco v. Superior Court, 37 Cal.2d 227, 231 P.2d 26 (1951); Tex. R. Evid. 510(d)(5).
22. People v. Stritzinger, 34 Cal.3d 505, 668 P.2d 738, 194 Cal. Rptr. 431 (1983); People v. Florendo, 95 Ill.2d 155, 447 N.E.2d 282 (1983).
23. People v. Arcega, 32 Cal. 3d 504, 651 P.2d 338, 186 Cal. Rptr. 94 (1982); State v. Soney, 177 N.J. Super. 47, 424 A.2d 1182 (1980); Tex. Cr. R. Evid. 509.
24. *In re* Alvarez, 342 So.2d 492 (Fla. 1977).
25. McCormick v. Caterpiller Tractor Co., 85 Ill.2d 352, 423 N.E.2d 876 (1981); State *ex rel* Holman v. Dayton Press, 11 Ohio St. 3d 66, 463 N.E.2d 1243 (1966).
26. Shuman. *supra* note 6, § 10.05, at 234 (1986).
27. *In re* Zuniga, 714 F.2d 632, 636 (6th Cir. 1983), cert. denied 104 S. Ct. 426 (1983). *But see Ex Parte* Abell, 613 S.W.2d 255 (Tex. 1981).
28. State v. Andrig, 342 N.W.2d 128 (Minn. 1984).
29. Shuman, *supra* note 6, § 10.05, at 235.

Chapter 2

PROFESSIONAL ETHICS AND CONFIDENTIALITY

Contemporary medical ethics traces its roots to the writings of Hippocrates. Proponents of physician-patient, psychiatrist-patient, and psychotherapist-patient privileges or professional secret[1] have frequently rested their arguments, at least in part, on the promise of confidentiality contained in the Hippocratic Oath.[2] Expressly or impliedly, these proponents have suggested that this portion of the oath contains some venerable wisdom about medical confidentiality which has stood the test of time and has some obvious bearing on the subject of a medical privilege or professional secret. Although much debate has taken place over the merits of these privileges,[3] the use of the Hippocratic Oath's promise of confidentiality as support for this position has remained immune from the controversy, blessed with an apparent mystical sacredness.

The Hippocratic Oath, while not the first recorded code of medical ethics, is one of the earliest and most significant articulations of medical ethics.[4] It is thought to have originated in the Hellenistic world between the fourth century B.C. and the first century A.D. and to be one of a group of ethical works attributed to the physician Hippocrates.[5] From its original form to its present version, the oath has evolved and been modified over the years. Yet the oath's promise of confidentiality has remained substantially unchanged from its original version:

> What I may see or hear in the course of the treatment or even outside of the treatment in regard to the life of men, which on no account one must spread abroad, I will keep to myself, holding such things shameful to be spoken about.[6]

Is this portion of the oath an early recognition of the need to assure patients that their secrets will be kept to encourage them to seek treatment or to make candid disclosures that facilitate treatment? There is reason to doubt that is the major force behind the oath's promise of confidentiality.

The oath entails a promise to keep confidential two categories of information, that learned "in the course of treatment" and that learned "outside of the treatment in regard to the life of men." While the meaning of the former phrase seems relatively clear, the latter is more obscure and given to at least two interpretations. The more narrow interpretation suggests that the phrase addresses information learned during treatment, but not always relevant to treatment. If this interpretation is accepted, the physician is promising to keep confidential all information learned about the patient during treatment whether or not relevant to treatment.

The other interpretation that might be attributed to "outside of treatment in regard to the life of men" gives a literal meaning to those words. Outside of treatment, according to this interpretation, includes the physician's activities while not engaged in treating patients, but other activities in which the physician might engage "in regard to the life of men." If this broader interpretation is accepted, yet another question is presented.

The language of the oath, on its face, does not distinguish between the confidentiality to be accorded information learned in "the course of the treatment" and "outside of the treatment in regard to the life of men." Does this imply a common basis for the obligation of confidentiality in both cases. If so, what might that basis be?

Ludwig Edelstein, whose extensive research on Hippocrates is internationally regarded,[7] places the oath in the mainstream of the Pythagorean school of thought.[8] The Pythagoreans did not reveal their teachings to the public; instead they sought to limit the dissemination of their knowledge.[9] From that influence, it may be inferred that the obligation of confidentiality accorded information learned within and without treatment is grounded in both instances on some anticompetitive notion favoring the physician rather than confidentiality protecting the patient from unwanted disclosure. This contention is bolstered by the fact that what the physician sees or hears "in the course of the treatment" is not focused upon seeing patients or hearing what they say, but would seem to include what the physician learns from treatments observed as an aspect of his medical education as well.

Additional support for this conclusion is found in another section of the Hippocratic Oath. The oath includes a vow to the physician's teacher which contains a limitation on teaching others what the student has learned:

> To hold him who has taught me this art as equal to my parents and to live my life in partnership with him, and if he is in need of money to

> give him a share of mine, and to regard his offspring as equal to my brothers in male lineage and to teach them this art—if they desire to learn it—without fee and covenant; to give a share of precepts and oral instruction and all the other learning to my sons and to the sons of him who has instructed me and to pupils who have signed the covenant and have taken an oath according to the medical law, but to no one else.[10]

This vow, limiting disclosure of the art of medicine suggests an overall anticompetitive flavor to the oath which is consistent with an anticompetitive premise behind the oath's promise of confidentiality.

Beyond the specific language of the oath, the very nature of the Hippocratic physician's practice belies the notion that privacy attended communication between physician and patient.

> When the physician goes to the patient's home he is accompanied by his pupils and others, and there he meets the sick man's friends and relatives. The more communal character of life in antiquity permits any audience even during treatment, which lacks the intimacy that modern man takes for granted.[11]

Thus the suggestion that the promise of confidentiality reflects some ancient psychological insight about the importance of medical confidentiality is not supported by our understanding of ancient medical practice.

Other language in the Hippocratic Oath's confidentiality provision is ambiguous and implies another limitation on confidentiality. The physician pledges to keep confidential only that "which on no account one must spread abroad." Who is to determine this and by what standard? Much debate has taken place over the meaning of this language.[12] Yet one conclusion is certain, absolute confidentiality was not intended by the author of the oath. Some secrets "one must [not] spread abroad," perhaps because as a Pythagorean one must guard medical knowledge and some secrets may be spoken abroad, perhaps because of some conflicting duty to society.

The oath's promise of confidentiality posits that what is seen "in the course of treatment or even outside of the treatment in regard to the life of men" should be kept to oneself "holding such things shameful to be spoken about." To whom will spreading such things about be shameful? The patient, perhaps, but significant portions of the Hippocratic works concern physician decorum[13] and in that context gossip is as shameful to the physician as is a lack of frugality. Although this position may be cast in an altruistic light—patients will better trust and be more effectively treated by physicians who are law abiding, frugal, and tight-lipped—it is equally given to a concern for the physician alone in his quest for patients.[14]

Numerous other written medical codes that came about in the centuries after the Hippocratic Oath, contain statements about the confidentiality of patient information. Yet in these codes, such as the Indian Oath of Initiation for Students of Vedic Medicine contained in the Caraka Sambita,[15] the Hebraic Oath of Aspah,[16] and the Chinese "Thousand Golden Remedies,"[17] the language about confidentiality is contained in sections concerned with physician image or decorum. Thus the concern with confidentiality in these codes is as likely for the physician in his quest for patients as it is for the patient's need for medical privacy.

In 1803 Thomas Percival, an English physician, published his influential work, "Medical Ethics; or A Code of Institutes and Precepts Adapted to the Professional Conduct of Physician and Surgeons."[18] Percival's work is thought to be the first major advance in medical ethics since the works attributed to Hippocrates.[19] It addresses the confidentiality of patient information in two sections:

> Chapter I. Of Professional Conduct, Relative to Hospitals, or other Medical Charities
>
> * * *
>
> V. In the large wards of an infirmary the patients should be interrogated concerning their complaints, in a *tone of voice which cannot be overheard.*
> *Secrecy, also, when required by peculiar circumstances* should be strictly observed. And females should always be treated with the most scrupulous delicacy. To neglect or to sport with their feelings is cruelty, and every wound thus inflicted tends to produce a callousness of mind, a contempt of decorum, and unsensibility to modesty and virtue. Let these considerations be forcibly and repeatedly urged in the hospital pupils.[20]
>
> Chapter II. Of Professional Conduct in Private or General Practice.
>
> * * *
>
> I. The moral rules of conduct, prescribed towards hospital patients, should be fully adopted in private or general practice. Every case, committed to the charge of a physician or surgeon, should be treated with attention, steadiness and humanity. Reasonable indulgence should be granted to the medical imbecility and caprices of the sick.

> *Secrecy and delicacy, when required by peculiar circumstances should be strictly observed.* And the familiar and confidential intercourse, to which the faculty are admitted in their professional visits, should be used with discretion and with most scrupulous regard to fidelity and honor.[21]

The concern for the confidentiality of patient communications contained in Percival's Medical Ethics is evident. Conversations with patients in the infirmary should take place in a tone of voice that cannot be overheard by others, patient feelings should be a paramount consideration, and secrecy and delicacy required by peculiar circumstances should be observed. All of these admonitions suggest a profound concern for the needs of the patient and his concern for the confidentiality of the information communicated to the physician. Additionally, the anticompetitive concerns of the Hippocratic Oath seeking to limit the disclosure of medical knowledge generally are implicitly rejected in Percival's Medical Ethics which urge disclosure of effective remedies.[22]

A potential limitation on confidentiality is, however, found in another portion of Medical Ethics. Chapter IV is entitled Of Professional Duties, in Certain Cases Which Require a Knowledge of the Law.[23] It admonishes the physician "that in judicial testimony the truth, the whole truth and nothing but the truth shall be delivered," and he is thus "under a sacred obligation to use his best endeavors that his mind be clear and collected, unawed by fear and uninfluenced by favor or enmity."[24] Nowhere in the discussion of this admonition or elsewhere in this chapter is the physician advised to limit or seek to limit his testimony, when it is sought, based upon the confidentiality of the information he has received. Instead one is left to conclude that the concern with privacy of patient information is left by Percival at the doors to the courthouse. This conclusion is understandable in its historical context. One quarter century before Percival authored his code, the English courts refused to recognize a physician-patient privilege and permitted physicians to be compelled to disclose relevant communications made to them in confidence by a patient.[25]

Percival's Medical Ethics was substantially relied upon by the American Medical Association in its first Code of Ethics adopted in 1847.[26] Confidentiality and its importance are addressed in two sections of the code which borrow heavily from Percival's language. The first set of italicized language set forth below is taken directly from Percival without change.

Chapter I.

Of the Duties of Physicians to Their Patients and of the Obligations of Patients to Their Physicians Art. I.—Duties of Physicians to Their Patients

* * *

> 2. Every case committed to the charge of a physician should be treated with attention, steadiness, and humanity. Reasonable indulgence should be granted to the mental imbecility and caprices of the sick. *Secrecy and delicacy, when required by peculiar circumstances, should be strictly observed; and the familiar and confidential intercourse to which physicians are admitted in their professional visits, should be used with discretion, and with the most scrupulous regard to fidelity and honor.* The obligation of secrecy extends beyond the period of professional services;—none of the privacies of personal and domestic life, no infirmity of disposition or flaw of character observed during professional attendance, should ever be divulged by him except when he is imperatively required to do so. *The force and necessity of this obligation are indeed so great, that professional men have, under certain circumstances, been protected in their observance of secrecy by courts of justice.*

Art. II.—Obligations of Patients to Their Physicians

* * *

> 4. Patients should faithfully and unreservedly communicate to their physician the supposed cause of their disease. This is the more important, as many diseases of a mental origin simulate those depending on external causes, and yet are only to be cured by ministering to the mind diseased. *A patient should never be afraid of thus making his physician his friend and adviser; he should always bear in mind that a medical man is under the strongest obligations of secrecy.* Even the female sex should never allow feelings of shame or delicacy to prevent their disclosing the seat, symptoms, and causes of complaints peculiar to them. However commendable a modest reserve may be in the common occurrences of life, its strict observance in medicine is often attended with the most serious consequences, and a patient may sink under a painful and loathsome disease, which might have been readily prevented had timely intimation been given to the physician.[27]

The American Medical Association Code of 1847 goes beyond Percival's Medical Ethics in a number of major respects. For the first time in a recorded medical code of ethics it posits the existing relationship between secrecy by the physician, disclosure by the patient, and efficacy of the treatment. Effective treatment requires full disclosure by the patient and this disclosure is a function of the physician's ability to keep the patient's disclosure secret. It is this theoretical relationship that will serve as the basis for successful medical association advocacy for a physician-patient privilege in the years to follow.

Another major change in the American Medical Association Code of 1847 is the recognition of the possibility of a limitation on compelled judicial disclosure—"professional men have under certain circumstances been protected in their observance of secrecy by Courts of Justice." New York, whose medical association was heavily involved in the adoption of the American Medical Association Code had, in 1828, enacted the first physician-patient privilege statute in the United States or any other common law jurisdiction.[28] It is therefore understandable that judicial protection of medical secrecy was on the mind of the Code's authors.

Five years before New York's enactment of a physician-patient privilege a committee of the New York State Medical Society presented to the society their draft of A System of Medical Ethics.[29] The fifth division, entitled Forensic Medical Policy, contains the following statement about confidentiality and privilege:

> The second rule is that of secrecy upon facts with which physicians become professionally acquainted, or are invited to ascertain; such as whether an apparent pregnancy be real; the gestation and birth of a child; its parentage, color and age; the judgement and treatment of syphilitic and gonorrheal diseases; the able or disabled state of a person, in limb or constitution; the fallacy of virginity and other circumstances, to the confessions of which a degree of shame and the idea of exposure is attached, and which are never mentioned but with an engagement to secrecy.
>
> This duty has been defined by comparing it to that of the Catholic confessional, which admits of no disclosures except in cases of treason or murder. This inference has been acknowledged by the judiciary of New York, and in its application to medical matters, admitted by that of Philadelphia, in the year 1800; and the Medical Society of the State of New York have adopted the same principle, so extended as to include felony. But this great privilege of the medical profession ought to be limited by discretion and regulated by a strong sense of moral duty; it should never be exercised to the injury of innocence or the violation of the rights of justice, or when it might operate to the dishonor or distress of families.[30]

Although most legal scholars date the first common law recognition of a physician-patient privilege with the 1828 New York statute,[31] this passage makes reference to judicial recognition as early as 1800.

The American Medical Association Code was revised in 1903 and again in 1912. The 1903 revision makes no significant changes in this regard,[32] however, the 1912 revision contains an interesting change.

> Chapter I. The Duties of Physicians to Their Patients Patience, Delicacy and Secrecy
>
> * * *
>
> Sec. 2. Patience and delicacy should characterize all the acts of a physician. *The confidences concerning individual or domestic life entrusted by a patient to a physician and the defects of disposition or flaws of character observed in patients during medical attendance should be held as a trust and should never be revealed except when imperatively required by the laws of the state.* There are occasions, however, when a physician must determine whether or not his duty to society required him to take definite action to protect a healthy individual from becoming infected because the physician has knowledge, obtained through the confidences entrusted to him as a physician, of a communicable disease to which the healthy individual is about to be exposed. In such a case, the physician should act as he would desire another to act toward one of his own family under like circumstances. Before he determines his course, the physician should know the civil law of his commonwealth concerning privileged communication.[33]

For the first time the code prescribes to the physician that a patient's confidences "should never be revealed except when imperatively required by the laws of the state." This change accomplishes several things. It recognizes that a conflict between confidentiality and legally compelled disclosure may occur and it avoids the necessity for the ethical physician to choose between adhering to professional ethics, contempt of court, or a suit for wrongful disclosure.[34] The physician is required to urge upon the court that the information is confidential and should not be disclosed, but if these arguments are rejected by the court the physician may disclose ethically and need not risk a contempt citation. Moreover disclosure pursuant to a court order arguably supplies an effective defense to any suit against the physician for wrongful disclosure.[35] This resolution of the physician's ethical dilemma was carried forward in the 1973 version of the American Medical Association's Principles of Medical Ethics:

> A physician may not reveal the confidences entrusted to him in the course of medical attendance, or the deficiencies he may observe in the character of patients, unless he is required by law to do so or unless it

> becomes necessary in order to protect the welfare of the individual or the community.[36]

The articulation of this principle is somewhat more oblique in the 1980 version of the American Medical Association's Principles of Medical Ethics which provides, in relevant part, "A physician shall respect the rights of patients, of colleagues, and of other health professionals, and shall safeguard patient confidences within the constraints of the law."[37]

The notion that the Hippocratic Oath's promise of confidentiality incorporates some venerable wisdom about medical confidentiality is, at best, subject to a reasonable doubt. At least three motives may have determined the oath's promise of confidentiality. It may incorporate some psychological insight into medical privacy, it may reflect a concern with physician decorum, or it may be an attempt to limit competition. Contemporary reliance upon this portion of the oath to support a relational privilege simply glosses over this difficulty in interpretating the oath. Its roots suggest it had little in common with the questions now raised by privilege or professional secret.

FOOTNOTES, CHAPTER 2

1. A relational privilege is a term used in common law jurisdictions to describe a limitation upon the power of courts to compel disclosure of confidential communications. Its civil law counterpart, professional secret, entails not only a limitation on judicial, but extrajudicial disclosure by the professional as well. In common law jurisdictions, an extra judicial duty of confidentiality is dealt with in other legal doctrines.
2. *See e.g.,* Dewitt, Privileged Communications Between Physician and Patient 22 (1958); J.L. Baudouin, Secret Professionel et Droit Au Secret Dans le Droit de la Preuve (Paris 1965); Knoppers, *Confidentiality and Accessibility of Medical Information: A Comparative Analysis,* 12 Revue de Droit Universite de Sherbrooke 395, 400 (1982). *See* Morissette and Shuman, *Le Secret professionnel au Qúebec: une hydre à trente-neuf têtes rôde dans le droit de la preuve,* 25 Les Cahiers de Droit 501 (1984).
3. *See e.g.* Chafee, *Privileged Communications: Is Justice Served or Obstructed by Closing the Doctor's Mouth on the Witness Stand?* 52 Yale L.J. 607 (1943); Hammelmann, *Professional Privilege: A Comparative Study,* 20 Can. Bar Rev. 750 (1950); Ladd, *A Modern Code of Evidence* 27 Iowa 213 (1942); Long, *The Physician-Patient Privilege Statutes Obstruct Justice,* 25 Ins. Co., J. 224 (1958); Morgan, *Suggested Remedies for Obstructions to Expert Testimony by Rules of Evidence,* 10 U. Chi. L. Rev. 285 (1944); Purrington, *An Abused Privilege,* 6 Col. L. Rev. 388 (1906).

4. The Hammurabic Code, dated at 1700 B.C., is thought to contain the first recorded code of medical ethics. G. Magno, The Healing Hand 44 (1975). However, it contains no references to confidentiality of patient information. Instead its concern with physician-patient relationships is the fee a physician (the asu) may charge for certain operations and the penalties for unsuccessful operations. G.K. Driver and J.C. Wiles, The Babylonian Laws ss. 215–23 (1952).
5. L. Edelstein, Ancient Medicine 6 (1967). The total collection includes the Hippocratic Oath, Laws, Precepts, and Decorum.
6. *Id.*
7. R. Veatch, A Theory of Medical Ethics 20 (1981).
8. Edelstein, *supra* note 5, at 37.
9. *Id.* at 47. *See also* J. Devogel, Pythagorus and the Early Pythagoreanism 64.
10. Edelstein, *supra* note 5, at 6. In addition to the oath, the works attributed to Hippocrates include The Hippocratic Law. Paragraph five of the Laws provides:

    Those things which are sacred, are to be imparted only to sacred persons and it is not lawful to impart them to the profane until they have been initiated in the mysteries of science.

    This language also suggests anticompetitive activities as a major force behind the premise of confidentiality. This interpretation is shared by Sissela Bok, the ethicist, in her book Secrets: On the Ethics of Concealment and Revelation (1982). To Bok, "the ritualistic nature of confidentiality in certain religious traditions has surely had an effect on its role in law and medicine. A powerful esoteric rationale for secrecy linked the earliest practices of medicine and religion. Thus, Henry Sigerist points out that in Mesopotamia medicine, like other sacred knowledge, was kept secret and not divulged to the profane; conversely, many religious texts ended with a warning that 'he who does not keep the secret will not remain in health. His days will be shortened.'" *Id.* at 123.

11. Edelstein, *supra* note 5, at 88.
12. Encyclopedia of Bioethics 174 (Reich ed. 1978).
13. Edelstein, *supra* note 5, at 36–37.
14. The Hippocratic physician is a craftsman. As a craftsman, he practices either as a resident or an itinerant; he may also settle for a while in some town, leave again, work in another town, or wander all over the country.

    When he is in a town, he works in his shop or in his patient's home. The shop is a place in which today one person, tomorrow another, plies his trade—not a hospital, not a consulting room in the physician's house. Sick people come to the shop for examination and treatment, or the physician goes to his patient's home. An itinerant physician works in the patient's house or has a booth set up in the marketplace of the town, or elsewhere, and practices there.

    The medical craft is not under any restrictions. Anyone can practice it without having to pass an examination and without being credited by any authority. As a craftsman, the physician of antiquity is classified socially as a businessman. While the modern doctor, in spite of the payment he receives, is not on the same social level as the other craftsmen who, like him, are paid for their services, the ancient physician is the equal of the other craftsmen and thereby occupies a low position in society.

    These circumstances determine the attitude of the patient to the physician and, consequently, the attitude of the physician to the patient. For the patient, the physician is not the doctor, the educated man to whose knowledge he defers and whom he recognizes as an authority in his field; on the contrary, the physician is a craftsman who must prove that he knows his business and that he is just as eager to do his work well as to earn money. The patient, therefore, tries to reach an objective judgment of the physician's qualities in order to distinguish the charlatan from the true physician. In his actions, the physician must take this into consideration; he must give people an opportunity to reach a decision about him and his ability. The authority that is essential in every treatment must first be established, and this means that the physician's behavior is dictated by nonmedical considerations to a much greater extent than are the actions of today's physician in his relations with his patient.

* * *

It is essential for the physician to prove himself and important for the layman as a future patient to know physicians and to understand something about medicine, and the form of life furnishes possibilities for the physician to make himself known beyond the individual case, to make a reputation for himself which frees him from the necessity of convincing people anew with each treatment. But when the physician is a stranger and unknown to the people, the impression he makes at the moment is all-important.

Id. at 87–89 (footnotes omitted).

15. The relevant portion of the oath, dated in the first century A.D. is as follows:

8. No offering of presents by a woman without the behest of her husband or guardian shall be accepted by thee. While entering the patient's house, thou shalt be accompanied by a man who is known to the patient and who has his permission to enter; and thou shalt be well-clad, bent of head, self-possessed, and conduct thyself only after repeated consideration. Thou shalt thus properly make thy entry. Having entered, thy speech, mind, intellect and senses shall be entirely devoted to no other thought than that of being helpful to the patient of things concerning only him. *The peculiar customs of the patient's household shall not be made public.* Even knowing that the patient's span of life has come to its close, it shall not be mentioned by thee there, where if so done, it would cause shock to the patient or to others.

Though possessed of knowledge one should not boast very much of one's knowledge. Most people are offended by the boastfulness of even those who are otherwise good and authorative.

Encyclopedia of Bioethics at 1732 (emphasis added). The Vedic of Aryuvedic School of Life is a Hindu School of medical thought. Charles, *Effects of Despotism and Freedom on Literature and Medical Ethics* in Transactions and Reports of the Royal Society on Literature in the United Kingdom 112 Vol. XXVII. The Unani system of Greek origin as modified by Arabic thought, contains a pledge of secrecy virtually identical to the Hippocratic Oath.

The overall flavor of the oath is more etiquette or decorum than ethics. It addresses the image the physician should project—not boastful, well clad, not sexually threatening and devoted to the patient.

Interestingly, the section also contains a "therapeutic privilege" permitting the physician to withhold information from the patient when the physician concludes it would be damaging to the patient. *See* Waltz and Scheuneman, *Informed Consent to Therapy,* 64 Nw. U. L. Rev. 628, 641–43 (1970); Somerville, *Therapeutic Privilege: Variation on the Theme of Informed Consent,* 12 Law, Medicine and Health Care 4 (1984); Canterbury v. Spence, 464 F.2d 772, 289 (D.C. Cir. 1972), cert. denied 409 U.S. 1064 (1972).

16. The Oath of Aspah, frequently referred to as the Jewish Hippocratic Oath, was written between the third and seventh century A.D. The section of the oath dealing with confidentiality also addresses physician decorum:

> And this is the oath administered by Aspah, the son of Berachyahu, and by Jochanan, the son of Zabda, to their disciples; and they adjured them in these words: Take heed ye kill not any man with the sap of a root; and ye shall not dispense a potion to a woman with child by adultery to cause her to miscarry; and ye shall not lust after beautiful women to commit adultery with them; and *ye shall not disclose secrets confided unto you;* and ye shall take no bribes to cause injury and to kill; and ye shall not harden your hearts against the poor and the needy, but heal them; and ye shall not call good evil or evil good; and ye shall not walk in the way of sorcers to cast spells, to enchant and to bewitch with intent to separate a man from the wife of his bosom or woman from the husband of her youth.

Encyclopedia of Bioethics at 1733 (emphasis added).

17. Sun Ssu-miao, often regarded as the father of Chinese medicine, authored "The Thousand Golden Remedies" in the seventh century A.D. Lee, *Medical Ethics in Ancient China,* 13 Bull. of History of Medicine 268 (1943). The section of this work devoted to medical ethics is entitled "On the Absolute Sincerity of Great Physician." Its discussion of secrecy is as follows:

> According to the regulations of medicine it is not permissible to be talkative and make provocative speeches, to make fun of others and raise one's voice, to decide over right and wrong, and to discuss other people and their business. Finally it is inappropriate to emphasize one's reputation, to belittle the rest of the physicians and to praise only one's virtue.

Encyclopedia of Bioethics at 913. Once again, the overall flavor of the section is decorum.

18. C. Leake, Percival's Medical Ethics 61 (1927).
19. Smithies, *On the Origin and Development of Ethics in Medicine and the Influence of Ethical Formulae in Medical Practice,* 3 Annals of Clinical Medicine 573, 584–5 (1924). Until the end of the eighteenth century, the medical profession looked largely to the Hippocratic works for resolution of ethical problems. Waddington, *The Development of Medical Ethics—A Sociological Analysis,* 19 Medical History 36 (1975). This is not to imply that students of medical ethics were idle during the middle ages. MacKinnen, *Medical Ethics and Etiquette in the Early Middle Ages: The Persistence of Hippocratic Ideals,* 15 Bull. of the History of Med. 1 (1952).
20. Leake, *supra* note 18, at 72–73 (emphasis added).
21. *Id.* at 90 (emphasis added).
22. Rather than limit medical knowledge, it seems that Percival would have the physician share knowledge of effective remedies:

> Chapter II of Conduct in Private or General Practice
> XXII. No physician or surgeon should dispense a secret nostrum, whether it be his invention, or exclusive property. *For if it be of real efficacy, the concealment of it is inconsistent with beneficence and professional liberality.* And if mystery alone gives it

> value and importance, such craft implies either disgraceful ignorance, or fraudulent avarice.

Id. at 104 (emphasis added). Other authors have found many nonaltruisic aspects to Percival's Code. *See, e.g.,* L. Berlant, Profession and Monopoly: A Study of Medicine in the United States and Great Britain (1975).

23. Leake, *supra* note 18, at 120.
24. *Id.* at 161.
25. Duchess of Kingston's Case, 20 How. St. Tr. 355 (1776).
26. Leake, *supra* note 18, at 50.
27. *Id.* at 219–20 and 222–3 (emphasis added).
28. Dewitt, *supra* note 2, at 15.
29. Transactions of the Medical Society of the State of New York 1807–31, 230 (1868).
30. *Id.* at 242.
31. Dewitt, *supra* note 2, at 15.
32.
> Chapter I.
> The Duties of Physicians to Their Patients
> Humanity, Delicacy and Secrecy Needed
> Sec. 2. Every patient committed to the charge of a physician, should be treated with attention and humanity, and reasonable indulgence should be granted to the caprices of the sick. Secrecy and delicacy should be strictly observed; and the familiar and confidential intercourse to which physicians are admitted, in their professional visits, should be guarded with the most scrupulous fidelity and honor.
> Secrecy to be Inviolate
> Sec. 3. The obligation of secrecy extends beyond the period of professional services; none of the privacies of individual or domestic life, no infirmity of disposition or flaw of character observed during medical attendance, should ever be divulged by physicians, except when imperatively required by the laws of the state. The force of the obligation of secrecy is so great that physicians have been protected in its observance by courts of justice.

Leake, *supra* note 18, at 240–1.

33. *Id.* at 257–8 (emphasis added).
34. The Statements of Policy Definitions and Rules of the British Medical Association contain a similar exception to the confidentiality requirement. Encyclopedia of Bioethics at 1758.
35. If the patient is a party to the suit in which disclosure is compelled, he would be bound, under the doctrine of collateral estoppel, by the court's ruling that the physician was under a legal duty to disclose. Even if the patient is not a party to the suit in which disclosure is compelled, it hardly seems likely that in the second action, for wrongful disclosure, the court would conclude that in the former action the physician was under a duty to disobey a court order and suffer confinement or a monetary fine.
36. American Medical Association, *The Principles of Medical Ethics,* 226 J. Am. Med. Assoc. 137 (1973). Psychiatry, a specialized branch of medicine, recognizes the Principles of Medical Ethics of the American Medical Association as its ethical code and has set forth annotations to provide guidance for the unique problems

of psychiatry. American Psychiatric Association, *The Principles of Medical Ethics with Annotations Especially Applicable to Psychiatry,* 130 Am. J. Psychiatry 1058, 1059 (1973).

Psychologists have developed a separate code with a principle of confidentiality that makes no reference to compelled judicial disclosure.

Principle 5
CONFIDENTIALITY

Psychologists have a primary obligation to respect the confidentiality of information obtained from persons in the course of their work as psychologists. They reveal such information to others only with the consent of the person or the person's legal representative, except in those unusual circumstances in which not to do so would result in clear danger to the person or to others. Where appropriate, psychologists inform their clients of the legal limits of confidentiality.

a. Information obtained in clinical or consulting relationships, or evaluative data concerning children, students, employees, and others, is discussed only for professional purposes and only with persons clearly concerned with the case. Written and oral reports present only data germane to the purposes of the evaluation, and every effort is made to avoid undue invasion of privacy.

b. Psychologists who present personal information obtained during the course of professional work in writings, lectures, or other public forums either obtain adequate prior consent to do so or adequately disguise all identifying information.

c. Psychologists make provisions for maintaining confidentiality in the storage and disposal of records.

d. When working with minors or other persons who are unable to give voluntary, informed consent, psychologists take special care to protect these persons' best interests.

American Psychological Association, *Ethical Principles of Psychologists,* 36 Am. Psychol. 633, 635 (1981).

37. American Medical Association, *The Principles of Medical Ethics,* 245 J. Am. Med. Assoc. 2187–8 (1981).

Chapter 3

PSYCHOSOCIAL THEORY AND PRIVILEGED COMMUNICATIONS

This chapter addresses the theoretical justifications for privacy that have been advanced to support the enactment of privilege statutes governing communications between psychotherapists and patients; that recognition of a privilege is a concomitant of privacy and that privacy is itself politically, ethically, socially, and psychologically important. Empirical studies examining these theoretical justifications, including the authors' studies, are presented in Chapter 5. Before examining these theoretical justifications here, however, it is first necessary to define privacy, confidentiality, and privilege.

Privacy is the claim of individuals, groups, or institutions to determine for themselves when, how, and to what extent information about them is communicated to others. Privacy involves a voluntary and usually temporary physical or psychological withdrawal of a person from the general society.[1] The terms confidentiality and privilege have specific meanings in a professional relationship. Confidentiality is a professional's obligation to guard the privacy of communications made in the professional relationship. Privilege is a patient's or client's right to limit judicially compelled disclosures by the professional person.[2]

I. Privacy as a Political Necessity

It has been argued that privacy is a requirement for the operation of a democratic society.[3] Without privacy, individuals are deprived of the independent reflection needed for political decision-making. Without privacy, there can be no convening of groups to discuss issues that might be inflammatory if more generally exposed, but that require consideration if the general welfare is to be promoted. From this standpoint, a need for privacy would not exist in a totalitarian state. Privacy would also not be a positive value in a totally egalitarian state, wherein all had equal access to everything. But, in a political system that emphasizes the value and uniqueness of individuals, privacy becomes an important value. The same is true in societies that choose to limit governmental power. Privacy is one means to reduce governmental power by allowing minor degrees of nonconformity to social norms, self-evaluation, and time to anticipate, rethink, and originate new ideas.

The thrust of this argument is largely immaterial, however, to a limitation on compelled judicial disclosure of psychotherapist-patient communications. First, the individual reflections or group discussion of political ideas contemplated has no necessary bearing on psychotherapist-patient relationships. Second, even if the reflection does, coincidentally, occur within the context of a psychotherapist-patient relationship, this argument wrongly assumes that political rather than personal issues will be the subject of therapy.

II. Privacy as an Ethical/Social Construct

It can be argued that just as each person should have the right to withhold his body and physical possessions from others, each person should also have the right to psychological self-concealment. Privacy as an ethical right of an individual asserts the value of individuality over community, and is generally accorded under circumstances when the needs of the community at large are not endangered. Under this rubric, it need not be argued whether privacy is helpful or harmful to the individual. Privacy is each person's right. Its consequences are less relevant than its exercise.

It can also be argued that privacy is a social need of human beings, for example, that a human need for protected psychological "territory" is equivalent to the need of other species for their own physical territory.[4] Each person needs a certain amount of psychological "space" that is analogous to a need for physical space. While the effects of physical crowding on species such as rats and mice has been investigated,[5] there is no data on the psychological crowding of humans. Many researchers have suggested, however, that families in which each member's need for privacy is not respected may produce or aggravate various forms of psychopathology.[6] In part, privacy can be conceived as a need for relief from maintaining ordinary social facades that are required to maintain productive work relationships or positive social relationships.

Privacy is needed to maintain the differing social roles necessary in all societies.[7] The medicine man in primitive cultures needs privacy to perfect his rituals and to protect the secrecy of his potions' ingredients. Parents withhold many aspects of their own relationships from their children while demanding much more disclosure by their children, both to protect their children and to reinforce their role as family authorities. Privacy is also an important part of intimacy. Sharing more of one's person with certain other persons creates a bond of specialness that could not be maintained if one were equally sharing with all persons. That privacy is a universal social need can be readily inferred from the fact that all societies recognize some form of privacy.[8] The amount of privacy accorded individuals differs from society to society as do the subjects that may be kept private, the circumstances under which privacy is allowed, and the purpose for which privacy is employed. Just as individuals balance their need for privacy against their need to share, societies balance the welfare of individuals against the welfare of the society as a whole.

In many situations, considerations of privacy have lost their original frame of reference and have been retained as customs or social norms. Thus, in Germany, much personal information must be disclosed to government officials, but photographing a stranger in public is potentially a criminal offense. In France, semi-open public toilets are used, but disclosures of patients' secrets to physicians is a criminal offense. Each of these attitudes of the state can be readily rationalized as for the greater good, but the incongruities are obvious.

Anthropological studies show that each society has cultural norms related to privacy. In the Kwakiutl tribe of the pacific northwest, material wealth was displayed; the greater the display and the greater the disregard for keeping the material goods that were displayed (they were usually burned in a public ritual), the greater one's social prestige and the greater the humiliation of rivals.[9] A Kwakiutl might keep the extent of his possessions to himself, but only to surprise and humiliate a rival in a public display. By contrast, good fortune was concealed in turn-of-the century eastern European shtetls for fear of bringing about the evil eye and subsequently misfortune.

Dobu tribesmen, whose island is near New Guinea, used privacy as a means to engage in socially sanctioned theft from and cheating of fellow tribesmen. While the Dobu were very prudish about exposing their sexual organs, boys were allowed to have sexual relations with girls in girls' family huts. The parents pretended not to notice until a boy, by tarrying too long, allowed himself to be "caught" and thereby betrothed.[10]

At times, societies set aside accepted norms of individual privacy for the common good, whether the factor that establishes what is in the common good is based on emotion or reason. For example, when the citizens of seventeenth and eighteenth century New England thought themselves beset by evil spirits and thought that the community as a whole was endangered by the presence of witches, individual citizens were no longer accorded the privacy they had formerly been allowed. When suspected witches refused to state if they had consorted with the devil, they were tortured. If they confessed, they died at the stake. If they did not, they were tortured until they died.[11] Thus, the community chose to rid itself of an imaginary danger to all rather than respect the privacy of particular religious practices.

The management of infectious disease offers a dilemma that falls more within the realm of reason. Physicians are required by law to report certain infectious diseases. In some cases, it is merely for statistical purposes. In the case of tuberculosis, it is to permit or require treatment of the primary case and infected contacts. Before the development of modern antibiotics, diagnosed tuberculars and lepers were often deprived of their liberty to protect the community from infection. This precaution was justified with active tuberculars whose sputum was laden with tubercle bacilli. The isolation of lepers was more related to horror of the disease. The actual contagiousness of leprosy is quite low.

There are quantitative and qualitative differences in privacy in all societies, but in no society is privacy accorded uniformly, as noted earlier in mentioning several contemporary societal norms. The people of the United States feel very strongly about individual privacy, and legislative safeguards or rights of personal privacy, equivalent to taboos against invasion of privacy in more primitive cultures have been enacted by the federal and state government.[12] However, these safeguards would not be necessary if the individual were always valued above society.

The roots of American concerns about privacy are multiple and complex. They probably stem in part from our emphasizing the worth and uniqueness of individuals—the recognition of individuals' autonomy as more important than their function as subunits of the larger society. The concomitant expectation, however, is that each person will disclose to the greater society what is required for the common good. Thus, all persons are relatively free to make moral decisions involving their relationship with the community at large, but also experience pressure to surrender privacy under certain circumstances.

III. Privacy and Psychological Development

Moving from the cultural to the psychological sphere, privacy is also thought to play an important role in the process of psychological development. The work of Mahler[13] with children of one to three years of age, for example, has led to the delineation of an important developmental process known as separation–individuation. Part of psychologically separating from one's mother is choosing what to tell her and what not to tell her. Having secrets–one's own psychological possessions–emphasizes sizes the child's sense of separateness and self-ownership. A sense of self, the healthy outcome of separation-individuation, can be aided in its development by many factors. Prominent among them is the mother's willingness to give up her children as an intimate part of herself, and to recognize her children as separate human beings by supporting their right to withhold and having the freedom, within limits, of decision-making based on their own logic or emotions. The failure of mothers to allow or to facilitate the process of differentiation leads to difficulty in distinguishing one's own thoughts and feelings from others. It thereby reinforces dependency, undermines the development of autonomy, and may lead to pseudoindependent behavior as a reaction to fear of engulfment, as well as equating intimacy with engulfment. The issue of privacy assumes great importance during adolescence, when the need of children to experience themselves as autonomous and their reaction to their developing sexuality cause them to avoid psychological and physical exposure to their parents.

It seems likely that competent parents are sensitive to the frequent changes in their children's need for privacy, recognizing that privacy should be granted at some times, but not at others. Competing needs for privacy and disclosure exist even in this context. For example, when a child's secret involves drug use or the ingestion of a poison, there may be need to violate the child's privacy. Usually, the resolution of such conflicts between parents and children is extrajudicial and does not involve privilege doctrines.

Failure to develop an adequate sense of self, partly due to parental intrusiveness, has been proposed by Kohut[14] as an important factor in the development of psychopathology. These theories will be dealt with in discussing the rationale for privacy in the psychotherapeutic relationship. Privacy is also a psychological issue for adults. It seems likely that each adult has an optimum level of privacy,[15] but the amount of control personal need to have over information concerning themselves varies from situation to situation, and is probably not a fixed personality attribute.

The importance of privacy in psychological development is largely immaterial, however, to limitations on judicially compelled disclosure of psychotherapist-patient communications. The decision of a parent to respect a child's privacy, for example, occurs outside the judicial context or psychotherapist-patient relationship and is unrelated to rules governing a psychotherapist-patient privilege.

IV. Privacy and Psychological Function

Privacy serves many psychological functions, from trivial to life-preserving; from avoiding the pain of self-criticism to avoiding life-threatening consequences of others knowing one's thoughts or actions.

At the most trivial level, privacy helps avoid the pain of ordinary social embarrassment over having had a foolish thought or having committed a foolish act. Self-criticism is unpleasant enough; the disapproval of others provides an additional source of discomfort. Furthermore, privacy enables the person who commits a foolish act to rectify the act, thus avoiding being labeled as foolish or stupid—an appellation that may follow a single act with disastrous consequences for self-esteem, interpersonal relationships, and work performance.

Privacy also helps in maintaining private belief systems that differ from the generally-held beliefs of a society or a peer group. If one's inner thoughts and beliefs are not exposed, they will not be contradicted, reasoned against, or thought odd, and one is less likely to think one's self odd. Many persons have beliefs they do not care to expose. Some of these beliefs are persecutory delusions. Some are milder self-deceptions, such as a sense of great personal power that is used to help maintain self-esteem. Other beliefs also have to do with maintaining self-concept, but in a negative way. A person who believes himself to be of little worth is unlikely to change that belief without first sharing it with others who hold him in high esteem and point out his positive attributes.[17]

Maintaining privacy can also help avoid the mistreatment that might result from others' prejudices, whether because a person has had an abortion, smoked marijuana, served a prison term, or does not believe in an afterlife. Mistreatment in these instances could include social ostracism, loss of employment, or even loss of life.

Finally, privacy aids self-deception by facilitating a splitting of consciousness. Splitting of consciousness was first demonstrated in the latter years of the 10th century. Breuer and Freud[18] and others noted that certain emotionally-disordered persons had amnesias—blank spots in their memories. They were unable to remember specific thoughts, feelings, and experiences. Freud[19] later found that this type of forgetting, which he called repression, is a normal process by which unwelcome or threatening thoughts, feelings, and memories are disowned and relegated to the unconscious part of the mind from which they cannot be retrieved by an act of conscious will. Freud based his theory of neurosis on this observation, and it is also the basis of psychoanalytic treatment. In the psychoanalytic treatment technique, patients are asked to say what comes to mind without the censorship they would ordinarily impose on what they think and say. Through this process of free association, analyst and patient begin to understand what has been repressed into the unconscious part of the mind. Free association is not the only means to discover what has been repressed into the unconscious part of the mind. That can also be achieved by hypnosis; which is sometimes used to help overcome more pronounced varieties of amnesia.[20]

Although the cornerstone of Freud's theory of neurosis was repression, Freud came to the conclusion that treatment directed solely at uncovering the contents of the unconscious mind was not effective. He found instead that aspects of what persons had repressed were played out in the relationship with the analyst, what he called transference, and that analysis of the transference was the curative element in therapy. Through analysis of the transference, what was repressed was brought to consciousness and worked through.

To overcome the self-deception that in psychoanalytic theory is part of neurosis, it is therefore necessary for patients completely to abandon privacy within the therapeutic situation and to suffer the embarrassment or other feelings that were avoided by the process of repression. The basic rule, without which analysis cannot proceed, is that patients agree to disclose all thoughts and feelings that occur during the therapeutic session.

V. Privacy and Interpersonal Relations

Social scientists agree that every person needs to disclose to some people[21] and to withhold from others.[22] Scientific studies support the need for personal disclosure as part of the process of social penetration and the development of intimate relationships.[23]

At another level, privacy is thought essential to insure personal dignity and freedom of self-determination.[24] In addition, privacy allows us to deceive others as well as ourselves. The element of deception brings the need for privacy into conflict with another need; the need of persons to know themselves and to know the truth about other people and about their universe as a whole. One means to learn about one's self is through psychotherapy. Truths about others can also be ascertained through informal inquiry or formal research. In some disputed cases, the search for truth leads to the judicial process.

A need for privacy at an interpersonal level can readily be understood. As Rachels[25] points out, the ability to maintain privacy allows us to create different relationships. Employer-employee, parent-child, and spousal relationships all differ in amount and type of personal disclosure. Employers generally disclose little of their personal thoughts and feelings and little of their personal lives to employees, thus creating a barrier that allows employers to treat employees largely as instruments functioning to a specific end. Parents generally know young children more intimately than they are known to their children, thus giving greater authority to the parent. The greatest intimacy usually occurs in love relationships, in which the sharing of each other's most private thoughts and feelings help foster the bonds of intimacy.[26]

The amount and type of personal disclosure create a power differential between people who work or interact together. The more personally open one is with another person, the more power is extended to the person to whom the disclosures are made. That person now has penetrated the discloser's social facade. Thus, his or her comments about the discloser carry greater weight than comments made by people who do not know the real or inner person. There is ordinarily an element of balance in intimate relationships. One member of an intimate pair knows just as much about the other's inner self as is known about his own. Psychotherapists take advantage of the power differential by maintaining a state of relative personal neutrality; what Tarachow[27] has called the therapeutic barrier. Psychotherapists' formulations about patients carry much greater weight than patients' might comments about their therapists, partly because patients have disclosed more of themselves. The therapist's privacy becomes a shield against what the patient might say and a lever that allows the therapist greater influence in the relationship than would exist if therapist and patient were social friends.[28]

While the arguments discussed above indicate that, in varying degrees, privacy is of psychological and social importance, it is difficult to see the relationship between a relative need for privacy and the absolute privacy that is conferred by privilege. In no social, political, or psychological context has it been shown that absolute privacy in any area is to the ultimate good of the individual or of society as a whole.

Privacy is always related to the importance of the values that are involved, but even societal and personal values vary in their importance in relation to context. A banal example of the influence of context on privacy concerns bowel functioning. Bowel functioning in adult humans is a private matter. However, it is a cooperative endeavor between infants and their parents, and between bed-bound persons of all ages and the persons who nurse them. Discussion of bowel function, while not an ordinary subject of social conversation, is a subject discussed in physicians' offices and between friends and spouses. Thus, it is apparent that privacy is context-related and not an absolute need. It is the issue of context that raises the strongest argument for privileged psychotherapeutic communication, as we will see next.

VI. Privacy and Psychotherapy

A variety of arguments, mostly utilitarian, are advanced for the importance of privacy in psychotherapy resulting in the need to recognize a privilege, as indicated in Table 1. The arguments against this need for privacy, opposing a privilege, are enumerated in Table 2. Both sets of arguments are considered below. Because of their similarity, the first two arguments for privilege are considered together.

A. Privilege Increases the Likelihood of Seeking Help
B. Privilege Decreases Delay in Seeking Help

These arguments are based primarily on fear of the stigma of being considered mentally ill by oneself or others. They state that if there were no absolute assurances that an individual's status as a psychotherapy patient could not be revealed, stigmatization and its negative social consequences would occur, deterring and delaying persons from entering therapy.[29] For example, a prospective patient's fear that prejudices in the job market about her status as a psychotherapy patient could result in failure to be hired or to be promoted might deter or delay that person from seeking necessary help.

Unfortunately for these purposes, the privilege laws governing psychotherapist-patient relationships from state to state do not generally protect against disclosure of a person's status as a patient unless by so doing the substance of the communication would be revealed.[30] The protection is only against disclosure of the information communicated. Indeed, to claim the privilege, it must be first shown that a psychotherapist-patient relationship exists.[31]

This premise also fails to take into account the use of insurance to pay for therapy. Thus, regardless of privilege, patients who make use of third party payors disclose the fact that they are psychotherapy patients. In addition, most third party payors require that a diagnosis be submitted to justify the frequency and duration of the treatment. Some persons may pay for therapy themselves to insure their privacy, but because of the high cost involved, it is likely that most persons who have insurance use it.

C. Privilege Increases Patient Disclosure and Effectiveness of Therapy

This argument is based on the premise that complete disclosure by patients to their therapists, absolute trust by patients in their therapists, and the avoidance of active interference by therapists in patients' lives are necessary for effective psychotherapy. The argument for the need for total disclosure by patient to therapist is based on the psychoanalytic model of psychotherapy and the concept of resistance. In Freud's words:

> We pledge him to obey the fundamental rule of analysis, which is henceforward to govern his behavior toward us. He is to tell us not only what he can authentically and willingly, what will give him relief like a confession, but everything else as well that his self observation yields him, everything that comes into his head, even if it is disagreeable for him to say it even if it seems unimportant or actually nonsensical.[32]

Freud based his technique on the premise that certain types of mental disorder called neuroses result from rekindling of emotional conflicts experienced during childhood. These conflicting drives or wishes are pushed or held in the unconscious part of the mind by an active process that he called repression. Repression takes place because the drives or wishes were experienced by the rational part of the mind (the ego) and the part of the mind that dictates our moral standards (the superego) as dangerous. Psychoanalysis seeks to bring the repressed conflicting elements into consciousness, thus exposing them to the influence of reason and enabling them to be worked through. The chief obstacle to this process Freud called resistance—a variety of mechanisms employed by the ego to maintain repression. Psychoanalysts deal with resistance by the use of free association (the fundamental rule described above) and interpretation.[33] Material from the unconscious seeps through if patients follow the fundamental rule, and its disguise is then penetrated by interpretation. In Freud's view, withholding information from the therapist potentially enhanced resistance and helped to block the therapeutic process, which is basically the removal of resistance to discovering what has been repressed.[34] Unless the patient is certain that the therapist can have no authority over him, for example, through disclosure of his communication in court, the resistance to full disclosure cannot be overcome.[35] The patient's complete trust in the therapist can only come about if the patient alone holds the key to disclosure of what has been revealed in therapy.

While this line of reasoning makes theoretical sense concerning psychoanalysis, it is not applied in practice. The analysts of analytic trainees report on their trainees' progress. If insurance is used to help defray the cost of psychoanalysis, a diagnosis must be disclosed to the payor. Analysts also discuss their cases in conferences and in print, sometimes to the dismay of patients who are sufficiently well known that their identity is guessed.

The most damaging argument against using the Freudian model as the basis for a psychotherapist-patient privilege is that psychoanalysis is a relatively rare form of psychotherapy. As a treatment requiring 4–5 sessions per week and having a duration of 4–7 years, it obviously cannot be widely employed. None of the many other techniques of psychotherapy presently employed requires total disclosure to the therapist. Many of the techniques, such as group and family therapy, actually break down barriers of secrecy between individuals.[36] Most individual therapies often focus on here-and-now aspects of daily living and do not conceptualize repression and resistance as such. In fact, exploration of unconscious mental processes is actually contraindicated in the psychotherapy of many emotional disorders.[37]

D. Privilege Averts Premature Termination of Therapy

This argument posits that the therapist's disclosure of confidential patient communications will destroy the trust necessary for an effective therapeutic relationship, thereby causing its premature termination. Despite this contention, it is noteworthy that psychotherapists have not generally advocated an absolute privilege.[38] Instead, they have recognized a variety of situations in which disclosure should occur without the patient's consent. The implication is that even psychotherapists think that certain societal concerns are more important than those protected by privilege.

E. Privilege Prevents Harm to Patients by Therapists' Testimony

There are two assumptions underlying this premise. The first is that what therapists might say could be innately damaging to patients' self esteem; that patients' worse fears are true their therapists are indeed judging them harshly. The other premise is that a damaging fact may be revealed, whether directly relevant to the legal issue at hand or not. This is exemplified by a psychiatrist disclosing a spouse's extramarital affair in a child custody case. The fact of the affair, whether relevant or not to the parent's ability to parent adequately, may be construed by judge or jury as evidence of general untrustworthiness or immorality. The assumption that without the therapist's testimony this information would not be revealed is based on the belief that information about events such as extramarital affairs is not also available from sources other than the therapist. If this information is available from sources other than the therapist. If this information is available from other sources the therapist serves only to cooroborate this information.

F. Other Arguments For Privilege

Another argument for limiting compelled judicial disclosure of patient-therapist communications is that what patients tell their therapists is distorted by the unconscious mechanisms at play when the material is disclosed, and may not be true. Thus, a scene first reported as a rape may turn out later to have been a fantasied rape. The opposite may also be true; an act that was initially reported as tender may be reported later as violent and traumatic. A patient's first account of an event as a rape may be an unconscious attempt to stimulate the therapist's sympathies. A later report of such an experience as an act of mutual consent may be intended to stir the therapist's jealousy. Because therapists can never be certain of patient's unconscious motivation for presenting certain material and for presenting it in the light that they do, what therapists learn from their patients can never be construed as a true account until (possibly) years later, when all the potentially distorting elements have been thoroughly examined.[39]

Another argument for privilege stems from a Freudian-based view is that patients in therapy can never give true consent. They may consent to disclosure out of a notion that it will please their therapist when such a disclosure is actually not in their own best interest. Or, they may agree to disclosure because they have an unconscious wish for punishment that would be gratified by revealing some aspect of themselves. In short, it is theorized that the strength of unconscious forces is so great that when it comes to therapy-related disclosures, patients might do themselves and their therapy great harm if even allowed a choice about disclosure.

Theoretical arguments for privilege also stem from other psychological points of view. Reasoning from the standpoint that effective psychotherapy must successfully rework issues of basic trust that are part of the earliest mother-child relationship, Uchill[40] argues that confidentiality must be absolute. She maintains that this is the only way in which enough trust, security, and stability can occur to develop sufficient emotional strength for psychotherapeutic work.

A final argument for not allowing testimony concerning information received in the course of therapy is that patients are more likely to maintain disabling symptoms if their therapists can testify for them. From this point of view, not only would the unconscious process of resistance be abetted, but therapy could also be a means to reinforce emotional symptoms through providing financial compensation. Receiving compensation or being relieved of responsibility for functioning at home or at work further reduces motivation for self-examination and self-help.

G. Arguments Against Privilege

The principal arguments in opposition to privilege deny the role of privilege in psychotherapy and point up the loss of probative evidence in judicial proceedings occasioned by the recognition of a privilege. Minimization of the role of the privilege in psychotherapy has often been supported by challenges to describe the differences in psychotherapy in jurisdictions which do and do not recognize a privilege. Slovenko[41] argues that the public is primarily concerned about the delivery, quality, and cost of health care, and is only marginally concerned about privacy. He agrees that patients may disclose less in the absence of privilege, but states that trust, not absolute confidentiality, is the cornerstone of psychotherapy. He opines that talking or writing about patients without their knowledge or consent is a breach of trust. Imposing external control when self-control breaks down is not a breach of trust when it does not involve deception. He indicates[42] that violation of confidentiality is the rule for persons who are treated by therapists in training and that confidentiality constraints defeat research. Lowental[43] points out that psychotherapists frequently violate patients' confidences in discussing cases with supervisors when in training and with peers when in practice.

Chafee[44] has stated that there is no substantial evidence that treatment of patients is hindered in states without privilege. Appelbaum[45] argues that most environments, including confidentiality, are less than ideal. He indicates that agreeing with severely self-destructive persons that confidentiality should be perfect fails to acknowledge the real need for information about them to be shared with appropriate people and may help patients to avoid facing the destructive manner in which they conduct their lives.

A frequently overlooked factor in considerations of privilege is the discomfort and embarrassment of the professional who is called to reveal information about a patient in an adversarial proceeding. With rare exceptions, mental health professionals, like all other witnesses, find it extremely disagreeable to be subjected to examination in a forum with rules foreign to their own professional norms. They lose treatment hours while waiting to appear as witnesses, become subject to an unpredictable courtroom schedule, and face attorneys whose job is to minimize their expertise and credibility. Yet, class exclusion from testifying on this basis raises serious problems of elitism.

Finally, it has been argued that the press for privilege by the medical profession is primarily based on professional jealousy of the legal profession.[46]

VII. Discussion

There is substantial disagreement about the extent of confidentiality required for effective therapy, with some psychiatrists arguing for absolute confidentiality, and others for lesser degrees of confidentiality. Plaut[47] has suggested three-tiered confidentiality; one level for involuntarily-hospitalized patients, another for patients whose fees are paid by third parties, and the most complete level for patients in psychoanalysis who pay their own bills.

The question of the relationship between patients' complete openness and the quality of their treatment has yet to be established. The argument that what patients tell their therapists is distorted by unconscious processes is equally true of all forms of evidence. Every person's perceptions are colored by unconscious fantasies and motivations. The law takes this into account by vehicles such as the hearsay rule which is designed to allow juries to decide after hearing the declarant that the likelihood that any statement introduced is credible. There is no more reason to exclude what was revealed in therapy than what was revealed to a policeman at the scene of an alleged crime.

Some merit may be found in the argument for absolute confidentiality that patients may allow or encourage disclosures that are destructive to them. Patients and therapists have been known to engage in mutually destructive acts, including sexual intimacy.[48] Conversely, the argument that ambulatory patients, as opposed to severely mentally ill hospitalized patients, cannot judge what is in their best interest is troubling. As indicated above, transferences and other unconscious forces affect all relationships. A basic difference between a psychotherapeutic relationship and other working relationships is that therapists take probable unconscious forces into account, and attempt to use them for patients' benefit. The assumption that the therapeutic relationship so disrupts patients' sensibilities that they cannot make judgments for themselves is false. Therapists do not make all of their patients' decisions for them, even with hospitalized patients.

There is little doubt that some persons will attempt to use testimony concerning their emotional or mental condition to maintain a state of disability or to gain unwarranted compensation. However, one is entitled to care and compensation for a legitimate disability. It seems more reasonable to deal with malingering or secondary gain-seeking through allowing mental health professionals' testimony instead of excluding it.

Tables 1 and 2 summarize the arguments for and against a psychotherapist-patient privilege. The review of the literature summarized above leaves most of these arguments poorly supported and most questions unsatisfactorily answered.

In Chapter 5, the results of the authors' studies of these arguments for privilege are discussed in the hope of shedding further light on this complex issue.

REFERENCES

1. A. Westin, Privacy and Freedom 31 (1967).
2. Group for the Advancement of Psychiatry, Confidentiality and Privileged Communication in the Practice of Psychiatry, Report 45 (1960).
3. Westin *supra* note 1, at 32–39.
4. R. Ardrey, The Territorial Imperative (1966).
5. Friedman, Glasgow, and Ader, *Psychosocial Factors Modifying Host Resistance to Experimental Infections,* 164 Ann. N.Y. Acad. Sci. 381–393 (1969).
6. W. Beavers, Psychotherapy and Growth: A Family Systems Perspective 194–196 (1977).
7. R.R. Murphy, *Social Distance and the Veil,* 66 Am. Anthropologist 1257 (1964).
8. S. Bok, Secrets: On the Ethics of Concealment and Revelation 22–26 (1982).
9. R. Benedict, Patterns of Culture 193 (1959).
10. *Id.* at 133–134.
11. G. Zilboorg, A History of Medical Psychology 212 (1940).
12. Jackson, *Privacy and Society,* 35 The Humanist 30–32 (1975).
13. M. Mahler, The Selected Papers of Margaret S. Mahler, M.D., vol. 2, Separation individuation 49–57 (1979).
14. H. Kohut, The Analysis of the Self 65–66 (1971).
15. Bates, *Privacy—A Useful Concept?,* 42 Social Forces 429 (1964).
16. S. Jourard, Self-Disclosure: An Experimental Analysis of the Transparent Self 5 (1971).
17. V. Derlega and A. Chaikin, Sharing Intimacy 8 (1975).
18. J. Breuer and S. Freud, Standard Edition of the Studies on Hysteria 12, in Complete Psychological Works of Sigmund Freud. Volume 2, (J. Strachey ed. 1957). (Originally published in 1895.)
19. S. Freud, New Introductory Lectures in Psychoanalysis, in Standard Edition of the Complete Psychological Works of Sigmund Freud, Vol. 22 1–82 (J. Strachey ed. 1964).
20. H. Crasilneck and J. Hall, Clinical Hypnosis 234 (1975).
21. D. Taylor, in Self-Disclosure 110–150 (G. Chelune eds. 1979).

22. Ruebhausen and Brim, *Privacy and Behavioral Research,* 21 Am. Psychol. 423 (1966).
23. Altman and Taylor, *Reciprocity of Interpersonal Exchange,* 3 Journal for Theory of Social Behavior 249 (1973).
24. Clark, Berelson, Blorestein, et al, *Privacy and Behavioral Research: Preliminary Summary of the Report of the Panel on Privacy and Behavioral Research,* 155 Science 535 (1967).
25. Rachel, *Why Privacy is Important,* 4 Philosophy and Public Affairs 323 (1975).
26. Weiner, *Health and Pathological Love: Psychodynamic Views,* in On Love and Loving 114–132 (K.S. Pope ed. 1980).
27. S. Tarachow, An Introduction to Psychotherapy 8–10 (1963).
28. M. Weiner, Therapist Disclosure 99–102 (2nd. ed. 1983).
29. Slovenko and Usdin, *The Psychiatrist and Privileged Communication,* 4 Arch. Gen. Psych. 25 (1961).
30. C. McCormick, Handbook in the Law of Evidence §9, at 215–216 (2nd ed 1962).
31. *See e.g.,* Fed. R. Evid. 104 a & c.
32. S. Freud, *An outline of psychoanalysis,* in 141 Standard Edition of the Complete Psychological Works of Sigmund Freud Vol. 23 (J. Strachey ed. 1964).
33. R. Greenson, The Technique and Practice of Psychoanalysis 32–33 (1967).
34. *Id.* at 59–66.
35. Dubey, *Confidentiality as a Requirement of the Therapist: Technical Necessities for Absolute Privilege in Psychotherapy,* 131 Am. J. Psych. 1093 (1974).
36. I. Glick and D. Kessler, Marital and Family Therapy 308 (2nd 3d. 1980).
37. M. Weiner, Practical Psychotherapy 174 (1986).
38. American Psychiatric Association. *Model Law Based on Confidentiality of Health and Social Service Records,* 135 Am. J. of Psych. 138 (1979).
39. *Psychonalyst Subpoenaed,* 2 Lancet 785–786 (1965).
40. Uchill, *Deviation From Confidentiality and the Therapeutic Holding Environment,* 7 Int'l Journal of Psychoanalytic Psychotherapy 208 (1978).
41. Slovenko, *On Confidentiality,* 12 Contemporary Psychoanalysis 109 (1975).
42. R. Slovenko, *Law and Psychiatry,* in Comprehensive Textbook of Psychiatry/III, Vol. 3, 3043–3083 (H. Kaplan, A. Freedman, and B. Sadock eds. 1980).
43. Lowental, *The Vicissitudes of Discretion in Psychotherapy,* 28 Am. J. of Psychotherapy 235 (1974).
44. Chafee, *Privileged Communication: Is Justice Served or Obstructed by Closing The Doctor's Mouth on the Witness Stand?,* 52 Yale L. J. 607 (1943).
45. Appelbaum, *How Strictly Confidential?,* 7 International Journal of Psychoanalytic Psychotherapy 220 (1978).
46. J. Wigmore, Evidence (3rd. ed. 1940).
47. Plaut, *A Perspective on Confidentiality,* 12 Am. J. Psych. 1021 (1974).
48. Zipkin v. Freeman, 436 S.W.2d (Mo. 1968).

TABLE 1
ARGUMENTS FOR PRIVILEGE

Psychological

Need for privacy

Need for private communication

Ethical

Right to privacy

Right to private communication

Political

Privacy and private communication are essential aspects of democratic society

Treatment

Increases likelihood of seeking help

Decreases delay in seeking help

Increases patient disclosure and effectiveness of therapy

Averts premature termination

Prevents harm to patients by therapists' testimony

Prevents use of therapists to reinforce disability

TABLE 2
ARGUMENTS AGAINST PRIVILEGE

Social

Not a great public concern

Frees patients from the consequences of their acts

Precludes detecting harm done by therapists

Endangering third persons for the sake of patients' treatment places individual needs above society's needs

Psychiatric

Trust, not absolute confidentiality, is requisite for therapy

Confidentiality regularly violated in training situations and by third party payment

Impairs research

Imposing control when self-control is lacking does not breach trust if no deception involved

Deprives patient of benefit of testimony (as in disability claim, malpractice action)

Makes needed medical/psychological information unavailable to other treating persons

Legal

Interferes with courts' fact finding

Obstructs administration of justice

Courts' need for information from psychotherapy is so rare that legal safeguard not needed

Chapter 4

LEGAL FOUNDATIONS OF PRIVILEGE AND PROFESSIONAL SECRET*

The need for personal privacy in communications and the need for probative evidence at trials are like separate melodies within the same musical composition. Each has a distinctive appeal, yet there comes a time in society, as in a composition, for a counterpoint or resolution of these independent themes within the fabric of a single work. That resolution has taken many forms. Some legal systems conclude that the receipt of probative evidence at trials is more important than personal privacy in communications and therefore compel disclosure of private communications. Other legal systems reflect a balance in which personal privacy is more important than probative evidence at trials and, thus, prohibit disclosure of private communications. Still other legal systems have evolved a patchwork of rules and exceptions favoring privacy in one situation and probative evidence in another.[1]

That different legal systems have reached different conclusions on this complex question is not at all surprising. The failure of the decisionmakers to examine the origins of their choice of the proper balance and the consequences of that choice, however, is surprising. This failure was perhaps best identified by Professor David Louisell:

> It is my opinion that the current analysis of the privilege is unsatisfactory and is contributing to confusion in judicial opinions. . . . [M]uch more extensive and thorough study in comparative law should be undertaken, including Roman, Canonical and European law; I think the eastern legal traditions also should not be neglected. Such study should be directed not only to the problem of the extent of recognition of the privileges in each country, but also to the question of the ultimate historical roots and precise rationale of each privilege. Indeed, so far as I know, this latter type of inquiry has not yet adequately been performed even in our own common law area.[2]

Courts and legislatures in this country that choose to recognize or limit privilege do not, as they often assume, write on a blank slate. Other legal systems with histories much longer than our own have wrestled with this same conflict between privacy and the need for probative evidence. The experience of these other legal systems is important for many reasons, but especially as a vehicle for learning alternative approaches to this problem and for testing various assumptions upon which our own approaches rest.

I. THE JUDICIAL PROCESS

A. The Conflict in Policies

Judicial proceedings frequently require accurate knowledge of some past event to decide correctly an issue involving the potential loss of life, liberty, or property.[3] Because the event at issue has already occurred and some knowledge of it has been irrevocably lost, the decisionmaker cannot possibly determine what occurred in the past with perfect certainty. At best the decisionmaker might expect to learn what probably happened, and the probability that the decisionmaker will accurately find the facts increases as more relevant evidence is received. Rational systems of evidence, therefore, are structured to accept all relevant evidence in the absence of a strong policy justifying exclusion.[4]

One rationale that has been advanced to justify the exclusion of relevant evidence is the need to protect certain important relationships and the values underlying those relationships through a privilege or professional secret. A privilege or professional secret permits its holder to prevent the discovery or introduction in judicial proceedings of confidential relational communications. Because this may result in the exclusion of highly probative evidence, there is a potential conflict with the use of judicial proceedings to resolve disputes accurately.[5]

The analytical approaches to resolving this conflict tend to fall into two different schools—utilitarian or instrumental and humanistic or deontological.[6] The utilitarian approach to privilege is represented by the views of Dean Wigmore. Wigmore viewed privileges as an obstruction to the truth-finding process that must be justified by its benefit to an important relationship. He thus imposed four requirements for recognition of a relational privilege:

(1) The communications must originate in a *confidence* that they will not be disclosed.

(2) This element of *confidentiality must be essential* to the full and satisfactory maintenance of the relation between the parties.
(3) The *relation* must be one which in the opinion of the community ought to be sedulously *fostered.*
(4) The *injury* that would inure to the relation by the disclosure of the communications must be *greater than the benefit* thereby gained for the correct disposal of the litigation.[7]

The utilitarian approach, which considers the utility of a privilege to the relationship it seeks to protect and the relationship's worth to society, raises empirical questions: Does the relationship originate in a confidence that communications will not be disclosed; is confidentiality essential to the fulfillment of the relationship? Thus utilitarian based arguments for privilege are, at least in theory, subject to empirical validation.[8]

The humanistic approach to privilege, which often relies on the writings of Professor David Louisell, views privilege as a protection of "significant human values in the interest of the holders of the privilege and . . . the fact that the existence of these guarantees sometimes results in the exclusion from a trial is merely a secondary and incidental feature of the privilege's vitality."[9] This school of thought focuses on the importance of the societal values embodied within a privilege, arguing that disclosure of confidences revealed in certain relationships is of itself wrong. Proponents of the deontological view contend that it requires a choice between competing values only and is not subject to empirical examination.[10]

The utilitarian argument favoring a physician-patient privilege is that it is necessary "to evoke and encourage the utmost confidence between the patient and his physician and to preserve it inviolate, so that the patient will freely and frankly reveal to his physician all of the facts, circumstances and symptoms of his malady or injury, or lay bare his body for examination, and thus enable his physician to make a correct diagnosis of his condition and treat him more safely and effectively."[11] Unless patients are assured that physicians cannot be compelled to disclose confidences, patients will not seek medical care or will not reveal to their physicians all the information necessary for effective treatment. This argument assumes not only that the patient is aware of the applicable law of privilege and considers it before consulting with a physician, but also that the patient would avoid treatment or withhold information necessary for effective treatment in the absence of a privilege.

Few contend seriously that these assumptions accurately reflect patient decision-making behavior in the case of physical problems.[12] Opponents of the privilege claim that people are not so shy or embarrassed about their medical problems that they avoid needed medical care in the absence of privilege.[13] Nor, claim the opponents, is there any evidence that patients know about privilege laws or receive more effective medical care following the enactment of a privilege.

Although utilitarian scrutiny of the physician-patient privilege in the literature has been harsh, the commentators have been more favorably disposed towards a psychotherapist-patient privilege.[14] These commentators assume that psychotherapist-patient relationships differ substantially from physician-patient relationships. While the absence of a privilege is not likely to deter a person with a broken leg from consulting a physician, the absence of a privilege would seem more likely to affect the decision of a person troubled by an extramarital affair to seek psychotherapy. Thus, it is assumed that effective psychotherapy requires an assurance that patient confidences will be kept inviolate. The assumptions underlying the utilitarian argument in favor of a psychotherapist-patient privilege are described in Chapter 3 and the empirical research inquiring into their validity is described in Chapter 5.

The deontological argument favoring the physician-patient and the psychotherapist-patient privilege are the same. Society should recognize the dignity of the individual by protecting these extremely personal relationships from unnecessary intrusions."[15] Disclosure is wrong, not because people will refrain from seeking care, but because it is wrong for society to intrude upon these relationships. The privilege represents to the deontologist a "right to be alone, a right to unfettered freedom, in certain narrowly prescribed relationships, from the State's coercive or supervisory powers and from the nuisance of its eavesdropping."[16] Thus, on the surface, recognition of a physician-patient or psychotherapist-patient privilege on this basis requires a value judgment: Should a society reject any intrusion into the sanctity of these relationships? This judgment does not appear subject to empirical scrutiny, but instead seems to turn on personal beliefs about the appropriate relationship between society and the individual.

This choice, however, is not entirely free from empirical underpinnings. Why should society reject any intrusion into the sanctity of these relationships and the resulting communications? What is the value of privacy? According to one highly regarded authority on the subject of privacy, we should value privacy because it is an essential ingredient of a democratic society.[17] Acceptance of this thesis requires more than a belief that democracy is a desirable form of government. It posits a causal relationship between privacy and democracy. Does more privacy enhance the democratic process? Should privacy be absolute to assure the purest form of democracy?

Legal systems have responded to the tensions posed by attempts to compel disclosure of confidential communications. These legal responses come from divergent legal systems and transcend substantial changes in the delivery of health care. Their origins and their evolution provide much useful information.

B. Legal Responses

1. Roman Law

The earliest reference to any relational privilege or professional secret in contemporary literature is the refusal of Roman law to compel the testimony of an attorney against a client during the pendency of the case.[18] This refusal of testimony seems to relate to the attorney's role as a servant, obliged to keep his master's secrets. Just as a slave could not testify against a master because the slave was a part of the family, and, therefore, a party to its mutual fidelity, so the attorney had a similar moral duty which the law recognized.[19] In addition, Roman law refused testimony offered by the attorney on behalf of the client based on the motive to falsify testimony.[20] The Roman rule barring testimony of attorneys, therefore, incorporated what we now call a relational privilege and a rule of incompetence.[21] The rationale for this relational privilege appears to be deontological: for society to compel a citizen to divulge a secret and thereby breach a moral duty is wrong.

2. Canon Law

Chronologically, the next reference to any relational privilege is found in the early Middle Ages when continental European codes excused and occasionally prohibited testimony from the clergy.[22] This restriction has its origin in secular recognition of the seal of confession and canon law.[23] Although confession during the third century occurred in front of the entire congregation, the Church had stopped its practice of public confession by the fifth century and instituted private confession.[24] The seal of confession was viewed as absolute, and betrayal by the father confessor impermissible. The seal of confession existed to avoid the risk of humiliation or prosecution for crimes that would deter confessions in the absence of the seal.[25] Canon law provided for the dismissal of a priest who divulged what he learned by hearing confession.[26] In some instances a greater sanction was extracted. Consider the following:

> At Toulouse, in 1579, an innkeeper murdered a guest and buried the body in the cellar: he confessed the crime to a priest who, seduced by a reward offered for the detection of the murderer, denounced the criminal to the magistrates; under torture the culprit confessed the crime, adding that none but the confessor could have betrayed him; an investigation ensued, which resulted in the Parliament of Toulouse releasing the criminal and hanging the priest, after he had been degraded by the bishop.[27]

With the exception of crimes or conspiracies against the king and his family, ancient French case law recognized this fundamental tenet of Catholicism and did not permit the priest to violate the seal of the confession by testifying.[28] And, although the French monarchy law did not generally impose criminal sanctions for breach of professional secret, the law did impose criminal sanctions in the case of violation of the seal of confession.

The Concordat of 1801 between the Catholic Pope and the French Emperor Napoleon was responsible for the establishment, respect, and free exercise of Catholicism in France. Because of the role of confession in the Catholic Church, French judges were required to respect and enforce the seal of the confession without exception.[29] Intrusion by the state upon this tenet of Catholicism was viewed as improper, a humanistic rationale for privilege.

3. Common Law

The modes of trial at common law in England prior to the fifteenth century did not suggest the need for relational privileges. They included trial by oath or oath helpers, trial by ordeal, trial by battle, and trial by witnesses.[30] Even in the case of trial by witnesses, jurors did not hear evidence so much as they reached conclusions based upon their prior knowledge of the case as members of the community.[31] Indeed, procedures for compelling testimony of non-parties did not generally exist. A witness who volunteered testimony was viewed as an unwanted intermeddler and subjected to suit for maintenance.[32] Gradually, the common law process changed. During the period 1450–60 equity courts recognized a subpoena that the Chancellor might issue on behalf of a plaintiff to a non-party witness.[33] A similar change did not occur in the law courts until the next century. In 1562–63 the Statute of Elizabeth abolished suit for maintenance against a witness and authorized penalties for a witness's refusal to attend after service of process and tender of expenses.[34] With the risk of compelled testimony came the need to examine the concept of privilege.

The first privilege to spring forth following the risk of testimonial compulsion was the attorney-client privilege.[35] Wigmore concludes that the attorney-client privilege was recognized in the reign of Elizabeth I and cites cases that follow closely on the heels of the Statute of Elizabeth.[36] Other sources refer to Wigmore's dating of the privilege and cite no earlier cases recognizing an attorney-client privilege.[37]

Did the common law's recognition of an attorney-client privilege spring forth independent of Roman law and its earlier recognition of an attorney-client privilege? One can answer this question, if at all, only through educated guess work. Although the Roman Empire included the territory now constituting England, Roman jurisprudence did not survive as a dominant influence on Anglo-Saxon laws.[38] English law did, however, borrow from Roman law.[39] The development of equity, for example, is thought to be based on the Roman *aequitas*.[40] English law also incorporated principles of the Roman law of slavery,[41] from which the Roman attorney-client privilege traces its roots. Although the earliest English cases recognizing an attorney-client privilege make no reference to Roman law or any other body of law as a basis for decision, the English jurists who decided those cases had ample opportunity to read and be influenced by Roman jurisprudence.

The decline in the importance of Canon law following the Reformation resulted in English law becoming more receptive to Roman law.[42] This period of receptivity coincides with the earliest recorded recognition of an attorney-client privilege in English law. Indeed, *Berd v. Lovelace*,[43] the 1577 decision cited by Wigmore as the earliest case recognizing an attorney-client privilege, was a decision of the Court of Chancery, which administered the English system of equity based on Roman law.

Most authors conclude that the common rationale for the attorney-client privilege was initially a "point of honor,"[44] gentlemen do not reveal secrets entrusted to them. With the shift in the factual orientation of trials, this basis for recognition of a privilege did not prevail for long. The adequacy of honor as a basis for refusing to give testimony was rejected along with a common law physician-patient privilege in 1776 in the famous *Duchess of Kingston's Case.*[45] The Duchess was tried for bigamy before the House of Lords. The crown sought to compel the testimony of Hawkins, her physician, that she had admitted to him the existence of an earlier marriage. Hawkins responded, "I do not know how for anything that has come before me in a confidential trust in my profession should be disclosed, consistent with professional honor."[46] To this Lord Mansfield replied, in what is now oft-quoted language:

> If a surgeon was voluntarily to reveal these secrets, to be sure he would be guilty of a breach of honour and great indiscretion; but to give that information to a court of justice, and by the law of the land he is bound to do, will never be imported to him as any indiscretion whatsoever.[47]

That the first known physician-patient privilege decision in English law did not occur until two hundred years after the first known attorney-client privilege decision is curious. This occurrence may be explained in several ways. First, because of the existing state of medical science, physicians may not then have been a reliable source of evidence. Second, attorneys may have assumed that physicians should not or could not be compelled to disclose confidential patient communications, and thus may not have requested the information. Third, attorneys may have assumed that physicians could be compelled to disclose confidential communications and thus may not have objected to requests for disclosure. Fourth, courts may have addressed this question prior to 1776 in decisions that remain undiscovered.

Was medical science likely to be of assistance to courts in the sixteenth and seventeenth century? Although the modern scientific method took hold in the seventeenth century, science still coexisted with a belief in sorcery, witchcraft, and astrology.[48] Thus, for example, wounds were frequently treated with "weapon salves" and "sympathy powders," cures in which the physician administered a salve to the weapon causing the wound.[49] The state of medical science revealed by this procedure suggests that medical testimony would be of limited assistance to courts. The question, however, is not whether medical testimony would help, but whether people believed it would help. No doubt in two hundred years medical historians will look incredulously at some medical testimony currently received into evidence. Just as this testimony is accepted as beneficial now, the following paragraph demonstrates that people utilized medical testimony in trials prior to the eighteenth century in the apparent belief that such testimony was beneficial then.

During the seventeenth century medical testimony regarding the cause of death was received into evidence in criminal trials.[50] And, in addition to whatever humdrum proceedings that allowed medical testimony, seventeenth century witchcraft trials permitted the introduction of medical testimony.[51] For example, in a 1662 English witchcraft trial two types of medical testimony were received. One physician testified as an expert that in his opinion the activities of the defendants were the work of witches.[52] Another physician, who treated a child cared for by one of the "witches," testified to the treatment he prescribed for the child.[53] Thus, whatever its actual or perceived benefit, medical testimony was received by English courts at least one hundred years prior to the *Duchess of Kingston's Case.*[54]

Did attorneys assume physicians could not or should not be compelled to disclose confidential information? Although it is unlikely that this question can be resolved with any degree of certainty, it seems unlikely that the legal profession assumed it improper to compel disclosure of confidential physician-patient communications. In the sixteenth and seventeenth century the practice of medicine in England was foremost a trade, not a profession of high calling.[55] Practitioners of law would have been unlikely to accord deferential treatment to most practitioners of medicine in sixteenth and seventeenth century England either as a matter of class reciprocity or professional respect.

Did English courts consider the question of a physician-patient privilege prior to 1776 though no evidence of such consideration has been discovered? The *Duchess of Kingston's Case* cites only one other case involving physician testimony in support of its rejection of a physician-patient privilege. That case, *The Trial of Lawrence Earl Ferrers,*[56] was decided in 1760. Thomas Kirkland, a surgeon, was called as a witness by the attorney general to testify to the wound received by the deceased as well as to statements made by the defendant and the victim concerning the source of the wound.[57] No objection to this testimony was made by the defendant or *sua sponte* by the court. Thus, the court made no ruling on the propriety of the surgeon's testimony. *Blackstone's Commentaries,* another source cited by the court in the *Duchess of Kingston's Case* discusses only the attorney-client privilege, infamy, and interest as excusing a witness from the duty to testify.[58] In the absence of the discovery of other cases, the most plausible theory for the lack of recorded consideration of the physician-patient privilege is that attorneys assumed that physicians could be compelled to disclose confidential communications and, therefore, did not bother to litigate the question.

Dean Wigmore viewed the *Duchess of Kingston* decision rejecting the physician-patient privilege as an historical turning point in the analysis of privilege.[59] After this case, according to Wigmore, the courts imposed a utilitarian test for privilege. Necessity, not honor, became the requirement for recognition of a privilege. The justification for attorney-client privilege shifted to necessity. Next, recognition of a physician-patient privilege was rejected as unnecessary because even in the absence of a privilege, courts believed that patients would tell their physicians everything necessary for effective treatment.[60] Indeed, the courts acknowledged that even necessity would not cause the recognition of a privilege in all cases:

> In the first place, the principle protecting confidential communications is of a very limited character. It does not protect all confidential communications which a man must necessarily make in order to obtain advice, even when needed for the protection of his life, or of his honour, or of his fortune. There are many communications which, though absolutely necessary because without them the ordinary business of life cannot be carried on, still are not privileged. The communications made to a medical man whose advice is sought by a patient with respect to the probable origin of the disease as to which he is consulted, and which must necessarily be made in order to enable the medical man to advise or to prescribe for the patient, are not protected. Communications made to a priest in the confessional on matters perhaps considered by the penitent to be more important even than his life or his fortune, are not protected. Therefore it must not be supposed that there is any principle which says that every confidential communication which it is necessary to make in order to carry on the ordinary business of life is protected.[61]

Courts in the United Kingdom have consistently refused to recognize a physician-patient privilege or any of its variants.[62] Legislative attempts to abrogate the common law's refusal in the United Kingdom to recognize a physician-patient privilege have also been rejected.[63] Although no privilege is recognized, the judge has broad discretion to allow a witness to refuse to disclose information if such disclosure would result in a breach of an ethical or social duty and if nondisclosure is not required to effect justice in the particular case. Judges have used this discretion in some cases to permit nondisclosure of physician-patient communications.[64]

Legislative abrogation of the common law has occurred in other countries which derive their common law heritage from England. In 1828 the State of New York enacted the first physician-patient privilege statute in any common law jurisdiction.[65] The revisers' notes reveal the rationale for that statute:

> In 4 Term Rep. 580, Buller J. (to whom no one will attribute a disposition to relax the rules of evidence) said it was "much to be lamented" that the information specified in this section was not privileged. Mr. Phillips expresses the same sentiments in his treatise on evidence, p. 104. The ground on which communications to counsel are privileged, is the supposed necessity of a full knowledge of the facts, to advise correctly, and to prepare for the proper defense or prosecution of a suit. But surely the necessity of consulting a medical adviser, when life itself may be in jeopardy, is still stronger. And unless such consultations are privileged, men will be incidentally punished by being obliged to suffer the consequences of injuries without relief from the medical art, and without conviction of any offense. Besides, in such cases, during the struggle between legal duty on the one hand, and professional honor on the other, the latter, aided by a strong sense of the injustice and inhumanity of the rule, will, in most cases, furnish a temptation to the perversion or concealment of truth, too strong for human resistance.[66]

The reference to Justice Buller's lamentation is from the case of *Wilson v. Rastall*,[67] a 1792 English decision of the King's Bench. Although the case turned upon the attorney-client privilege, in particular whether the defendant had consulted the attorney witness in his capacity as an attorney, Justice Buller's gratuitous observations on the physician-patient privilege were noted and agreed with by the New York legislature. Justice Buller stated:

> There are cases, to which it is much to be lamented that the law of privilege is not extended; those in which medical persons are obliged

> to disclose the information which they acquire by attending in their professional characters. This point was very much considered in *The Duchess of Kingston*'s case (a), where Sir *C. Hawkins*, who had attended the Duchess as a medical person, made the objection himself, but was overruled, and compelled to give evidence against the prisoner.[68]

The New York Medical Society's 1823 draft of A System of Medical Ethics contains a reference to an American judicial recognition of a physician-patient privilege during that same period. The footnote reference contains no case citation, but only the following: "The same principal was recognized by a superior court of Pennsylvania in the year 1800, in the case of a physician who refused to disclose his professional acts, against a defendant, in a suit for divorce on the plea of adultery."[69] This reference to an apparently unreported trial court decision is difficult to verify, but suggests that even in American jurisprudence, the New York statute was not written on an empty slate.

Following the enactment of the New York statute, a successful campaign of legislative advocacy in the United States ensued. By the 1950's roughly two-thirds of the states recognized a physician-patient privilege.[70] Then, in 1960, the Group for the Advance of Psychiatry issued a report that addressed the special need for a privilege in the practice of psychiatry.[71]

> Among physicians, the psychiatrist has a special need to maintain confidentiality. His capacity to help his patients is completely dependent upon their willingness and ability to talk freely. This makes it difficult if not impossible for him to function without being able to assure his patients of confidentiality and, indeed, privileged communication. Where there may be exceptions to this general rule . . . , there is wide agreement that confidentiality is a *sine qua non* for successful psychiatric treatment. The relationship may well be likened to that of the priest-penitent or the lawyer-client. Psychiatrists not only explore the very depths of their patients' conscious, but their unconscious feelings and attitudes as well. Therapeutic effectiveness necessitates going beyond a patient's awareness and, in order to do this, it must be possible to communicate freely. A threat to secrecy blocks successful treatment.

This report triggered other writings and advocacy efforts that led to the enactment of a multitude of psychiatrist, psychologist, and psychotherapist-patient privileges. Currently only two states, South Carolina and West

Virginia, lack a physician-patient, psychiatrist-patient, psychologist-patient, or psychotherapist-patient privilege.[72]

Other countries with a common law heritage, including New Zealand,[73] Victoria (Australia),[74] Israel,[75] Tasmania (Australia),[76] New Foundland,[77] and Honduras[78] have enacted physician-patient privileges. On the other hand, Canada[79] (with the exception of Quebec[80]), Australia[81] (with the exception of Tasmania and Victoria) and South Africa[82] have refused to recognize a physician-patient or related privilege.

The debate over the physician-patient privilege in common law jurisdictions typically turns on the utilitarian rationale for the privilege. The majority of commentators, including Wigmore, have concluded that the physician-patient privilege cannot survive scrutiny under this approach.[83] Those commentators that have examined a psychiatrist-patient, psychologist-patient, or psychotherapist-patient privilege have reached the conclusion that these privileges do survive scrutiny under the utilitarian rationale.[84]

Although the physician-patient privilege statutes in common law jurisdictions vary greatly, they do have certain characteristics. They apply only to judicially compelled disclosures. Professional ethics, rather than privilege statutes, govern noncompulsory extrajudicial disclosures.[85] The privilege requires for its application that a person, seeking treatment or diagnosis in contemplation of treatment, consult a licensed physician.[86] The communications sought to be cloaked by the privilege must have been made by the patient in a confidential context and have been pertinent to the treatment or diagnosis.[87]

These physician-patient privileges are not absolute. Their protection may be waived by the patient, who holds the privilege.[88] And, the privilege is not available in all proceedings. In certain proceedings that vary from jurisdiction to jurisdiction, the privilege's application is excepted. These exceptions include criminal cases,[89] workers compensation proceedings,[90] and will contests.[91] Typically the privilege is not available when the condition for which treatment or diagnosis was sought is raised by the patient to support a claim or defense.[92] When the parent-child relationship is at issue, an exception often applies to limit the effect of the privilege.[93] When a psychiatrist, psychologist, or psychotherapist-patient privilege is recognized, its requirements and exceptions typically follow those of the physician-patient privilege described above, varying only in the definition of the treating professional.[94]

4. Civil Law

In contradistinction to the English common law, French civil law recognizes a limitation on the power of courts to compel disclosure of confidential physician-patient communications. This limitation in French law, and that of other civil law continental European countries that recognize the same rule, is referred to as professional secret. Historians have traced the roots of the physician-patient professional secret in French law, le secret medical, to the attorney-client privilege or professional secret in Roman law.[95] When the territory now constituting France was incorporated into the Roman Empire, Roman law, including the attorney-client privilege, became the applicable law.[96] Subsequently, when the Teutons and other Germanic tribes invaded France, Roman law was displaced, and all traces of privilege or professional secret disappeared for several centuries.[97] The Roman system was replaced with Germanic and Frankish procedures based upon trial by battle or ordeal that did not require rules of evidence.[98]

Ultimately, a combination of events fostered a rebirth of privilege or professional secret. The efforts of the Church reintroduced Roman law in Western Europe when extensive research by Gregorian Monks led to the discovery of the Roman Digest.[99] The attorney-client privilege contained therein was then incorporated into the Decree of Gratian,[100] which served as the foundation for the Corpus Juris Canonici, or Canon Law Code.[101] Roman and Canon law, laden with the seed of professional secret, impregnated the substantive and procedural aspects of French secular law through a process of imitation and incorporation.[102]

Another factor that contributed to the recognition of a physician-patient professional secret was the importation of medical science into the Western Christian world by Jews in the eleventh and twelfth centuries.[103] This importation, after centuries of regression, occurred first in Italy and then in France. Domat, the great French legal scholar, traced the roots of the physician-patient professional secret to the incorporation of the Hippocratic Oath in the Constitution of the old Paris Medical School at the time of the rediscovery of medical science.[104] The climbing of the social ladder by the medical profession led to the profession's political importance and conferral of privileges by the ruling aristocracy.[105]

At the end of the Feudal Period both Roman and Customary law began to have a serious impact upon French secular law. Canon law courts used Roman law to deal with both church and secular matters, and such use slowly transformed French procedure, culminating in the sixteenth and seventeenth centuries. In 1670, the "Ordonnance of 1670" established a limitation on evidentiary sources and instituted the practice of hearing witnesses in court.[106] The first traces of physician-patient professional secret coincide chronologically with development of this new French procedure.[107]

French customary law developed rules excluding certain relational communications which were later extended to physicians. Borrowing heavily from Roman and Canon law, the customary laws of some French provinces acknowledged that breach of the seal of confession should not only be prohibited, but also severely punished, because confidences had been disclosed to the priest as a representative of God.[108] French customary law also recognized a limitation on disclosure of attorney-client communications.[109] The courts perceived those limitations on evidentiary sources as contrary to, and less important than, the goal of discovering truth at trial and, therefore narrowly construed them.[110] The development of professional secret in France, against the background of Roman, Canon, and customary evidence law, was slowed by the frantic desire to find truth, even through torture, by the authoritative political system, and by the French monarchy.[111]

By the sixteenth and seventeenth centuries physicians joined priests and attorneys in having a legal duty of confidentiality.[112] Breach of that duty gave rise to liability for damages from the financial and social consequences of the breach, but no criminal penalties were imposed.[113] While the duty of confidentiality did not translate exactly as a privilege, it did effect a limitation on judicial disclosure. Early French caselaw allowed members of some professions to ask the judge to be exempted from testifying if their testimony would reveal secrets learned in their professional practice.[114] With respect to the medical profession, that exemption was based on the risk of physician liability for damages upon breach of confidentiality[115] and the more general respect of these professional secrets. Two theories were utilized to warrant judicial recognition of these professional secrets. The first theory postulated that the physician and patient were the bailee and bailor of secrets. The second theory viewed the physician and patient as parties to a contract in which the physician promised to keep the patient's confidences.[116]

The struggle between the search for truth at trial and the confidentiality of professional secrets continued, and a leading legal scholar of the time described its status prior to the French Revolution in this manner:

> One cannot compel an attorney or a physician to disclose the secrets revealed to them by the client. . . . However there are some decision of the 'Parlement de Paris' mandating lawyers to testify about privileged matters, in light of the critical importance of their testimony in the search for truth. Marnac says that the ancient caselaw held that attorneys and other professionals could not be ordered to disclose secrets and confidences, but that now courts force them to do so; he adds that the most illustrious legal experts tried their hardest to keep the old position alive, but failed in their endeavor.[117]

Ultimately this see-saw led to the passage of article 378 of the French Penal Code of 1810, which recognized professional secret and imposed criminal penalties for its violation.

> Physicians, surgeons and other health officials, as well as pharmacists, nurses, and all other persons "bailees of secrets and confidences communicated" to them because of their status or profession, who will reveal those secrets, in all instances other than when the law compels them to disclose, will be punished with a term of no less than one month and no more than six months of imprisonment and a fine of no less than 10.00 and no more than 100.00 francs.[118]

Legislative history reveals the original rationale for this article.

> Should we not consider that disclosure of privileged information is a serious offense because—it shatters the reputation of the patient whose secret is betrayed—it destroys the patient's confidence in the physician, since this confidence has become more harmful than useful—it causes people to choose silence and mental or physical suffering rather than benefiting from educated persons' help—it portrays professionals, whose image should be one of therapists, counselors and men looking for the patient's best interest, as traitors?
>
> This provision is a novelty in our legal system. We would have wished that ethical considerations and tact would cause it to be useless. But how many times do we not see professionals, to whom secrets have been entrusted, sacrifice their duty on the altar of caustic humor, kid about the gravest matters, keep malice alive with indecent revelations, obscene stories, and bring shame and sorrow upon the patients and their families?[119]

The underlying concern expressed is protection of the patient's reputation in the community from the perceived danger of indiscrete physicians.[120] In early 19th century France a person's reputation seriously affected his employment, friendship, marriage, and social status. Disclosure of conditions such as venereal disease or organic malfunction was, therefore, a serious evil to be avoided.[121]

Since the enactment of article 378, commentators have advanced additional, albeit overlapping, rationales to support the professional secret. One such rationale is that revelation of confidences disrupts the "social order."[122] For example, revelation that a patient suffers from a communicable or genetically transmitted disease might disturb the peace of the patient's family, result in societal rejection of the patient, and thereby resulting in a weakening of the social fabric.

Another justification advanced for professional secret is the right of privacy.[123] According to the privacy rationale, the state's intrusion upon highly personal aspects of a citizen's private domain is simply wrong. Particularly during troubled political times, arbitrary disclosure of patient information threatens the right to privacy.[124]

Still another rationale advanced for the professional secret is that the physician is the "trustee by necessity" of the patient's secrets.[125] Proponents of this theory maintain that trust is conducive to the patient's seeking and receiving treatment. Thus, the patient must be assured that his confidences will be kept. A disclosure of confidential information would forfeit the patient's confidence in the physician, breach the physician's duty as trustee by necessity, and cause people with embarrassing diseases not to seek treatment.[126]

Because the initial rationale for the professional secret was the protection of reputation from small talk at social events, the draftsmen of article 378 focused upon garrulous physician behavior rather than judicially compelled testimony. Much confusion has thereby resulted in article 378's relation to the legal system. One major ongoing question is whether article 378 is absolute. Can the professional secret be waived? Does it permit exceptions? Proponents of an absolute professional secret contend that "if we examine the origins of the duty of professional secret we find that the interests of the community are considered just as important as the individual's need for privacy."[127] If disclosure is permitted, other members of the community may hesitate to make disclosures to their physicians.[128] Thus, the professional secret is not simply a right belonging to the patient that he may waive at his discretion. Rather the professional secret is a protection of the entire community and is therefore beyond the capacity of any individual patient to waive.

French law does not permit the consent of the victim to alter the character of a criminal offense.[129] The victim may not alter the policy of the criminal laws and society's power to punish violations. Thus, absolutists argue, the patient may not waive or consent to a violation of professional secret because the patient may neither abrogate the policy underlying the secret or limit society's power to punish violations.[130]

Those who oppose the absolute view argue that the privilege is designed to protect the interests of individual patients. Patients should be permitted to determine whether waiver will protect or hinder their interests. Proponents of this position argue that waiver by one individual will not deter another patient from seeking help since each individual realizes that waiver is his choice to make.

Although the absolute position prevailed initially, that supremacy has been tempered over time.[131] Only the criminal chamber of the French high court, the Cour de Cassation, has adhered to the concept of the absolute professional secret.[132] According to its decisions, the patient may not waive the secret's application even when the physician's disclosure would be exculpatory. Even in criminal cases, however, a gradual loosening may be occurring.

Conversely, the civil chamber of the Cour de Cassation has espoused a nonabsolute view of professional secret.[133] That court has permitted waiver of the secret when waiver would serve the patient's best interests. For example, waiver has been permitted to support a claim for disability benefits or to explain a party's unavailability at trial.[134] Similarly waiver has been permitted when it would serve the interests of the patient's family, for example, to support a challenge to the mental capacity of the author of a will.[135] And, the public order has permitted an implied waiver of the secret, for example, to assist the physician to defend a medical malpractice claim[136] or where the patient poses a serious danger to third persons.[137]

Article 378's protections apply both to information that a patient voluntarily reveals to a physician acting in a professional capacity and to information discovered or involuntarily revealed, sometimes called secrets by nature.[138] The earlier view was that the secret covered only information prejudicial to the patient. This view, however, has now been abandoned and the professional secret now covers disclosure of non-prejudicial information as well.[139] A violation of the professional secret statute exists whether the physician discloses the confidential information to the public or merely a single person.[140] Although malice was initially required to constitute a violation of the professional secret, this requirement has been replaced by a requirement of intentional conduct. Negligent conduct, however, remains insufficient to trigger a violation of article 378.[141]

The professional secret statutes of other civil law countries are not absolute. For example, Germany,[142] Switzerland,[143] Italy,[144] Belgium,[145] and Portugal[146] require a complaint from the patient to initiate prosecution. In addition, Italy and Portugal permit an exception to the secret when required by the public interest.

5. Comparison and Summary

The difference between what common law jurisdictions call privilege and civil law jurisdictions call professional secret is not merely semantic. Professional secret has a much broader application; it applies to the professional both in court and out of court. Common law jurisdictions leave extrajudicial disclosures to the realm of professional ethics and not to the realm of privilege. Professional secret, however, combines the common law concept of privilege with professional ethics, and thus establishes a criminal sanction for a violation of either.

Professional secret protects a greater fund of patient information. Privilege protects only information that the patient communicates to the physician; professional secret protects not only information communicated by the patient, but information communicated by other sources as well. Moreover, while common law courts require a close nexus between the communication and the treatment, civil law courts have permitted greater latitude on this question.

Common law jurisdictions always permit a voluntary waiver of the privilege by the patient, viewing it as any other individual right subject to waiver. Civil law jurisdictions do not always permit a voluntary waiver of the professional secret by the patient, often viewing it as a societal right rather than merely an individual right. Furthermore, although the rationales advanced for the physician-patient privilege and professional secret tend to overlap, the privilege tends to rely more heavily on the utilitarian rationale and the professional secret tends to rely more heavily on the non-utilitarian rationale.

Many differences in civil and common law procedures are explainable through the use of the inquisitorial or adversarial system and the use or non-use of the jury.[147] Hearsay evidence, for example, is freely admitted in civil law countries where juries are rare. Common law countries, however, limit the admissibility of hearsay because of a fear that juries will not properly evaluate it. The distinction between privilege and professional secret, however, does not turn on these procedural differences. Evidence of a confidential communication is not excluded, like hearsay in a common law jurisdiction, because the jury may accord it too much weight or be misled by it. Confidential communications may be extremely probative and unambiguous. Rather, confidential communications are excluded because the evil sought to be avoided is exposure to any unintended third party, judge or jury, in any context, adversarial or inquisitorial. Thus there is nothing inherent in the civil and common law systems that explains their varied approaches to this problem.

Common and civil law systems wrestle with the same tension between accurate fact finding and confidential communications. Despite their shared Roman law ancestry, their written approach to this tension differs widely. Yet, it is not at all clear that variations in existing practice are as wide as these statutes and cases might suggest. The study of judicial decisionmaking described in Chapter 5 reveals a remarkable similarity of approach in addressing compelled disclosure of confidential psychotherapist-patient communications in jurisdictions with widely varying statutes and caselaw. Moreover, the two systems are moving, from opposite poles, in a similar direction. The civil law system, beginning with an absolute limitation on disclosure of physician-patient communications, has evolved to a relativist approach by recognizing the possibility of waiver of and exception to the privilege. The common law system, beginning with no limitation on compelled judicial disclosure of physician-patient communications, has also evolved to a relativist approach by recognizing physician-patient privilege and more recently, psychiatrist, psychologist, and psychotherapist-patient privileges. And, the scope of these privileges is also limited by the possibility of waiver or exception.

FOOTNOTES, CHAPTER 4

* An earlier version of this chapter was published as Shuman, *The Origins of the Physician-Patient Privilege and Professional Secret*, 39 Sw.L.J. 101 (1985). Copyright, 1985, by Southern Methodist University. Reprinted with permission from Southwestern Law Journal.

1. Privilege, professional secret, confidentiality, secrecy, and privacy are words

used to describe these relationships and will be used throughout this article. Privilege is the common law term for a rule favoring privacy over probative evidence, and professional secret is its civil law counterpart. Privilege and professional secret are not, however, different words describing the same thing as these doctrines differ substantially in their application. See Section IIIB infra.

Confidentiality is the ethical duty of the professional, operating outside of the judicial setting, not to disclose confidential communications made by the patient or client. Secrecy is the expectation that a communication will not be disclosed. And, privacy is the ability to control revelation of information about oneself.

2. Louisell, *Confidentiality, Conformity and Confusion: Privileges in Federal Court Today,* 31 Tul. L. Rev. 101 (1957).
3. *See,* Shuman and Weiner, *The Privilege Study: An Empirical Examination of the Psychotherapist-Patient Privilege,* 60 N.C. L. Rev. 893, 904 (1982).
4. J. Thayer, A Preliminary Treatise on Evidence at the Common Law 530 (1898).
5. Testimonial exclusionary rules and privileges contravene the fundamental principle that "the public . . . has a right to every man's evidence." *United States v. Bryan,* 339 U.S. 323, 331 (1940). As such, they must be strictly construed and accepted "only to the very limited extent that permitting a refusal to testify or excluding relevant evidence has a public good transcending the normally predominant principle of utilizing all rational means for ascertaining truth." *Elkins v. United States,* 364 U.S. 206, 234 (1960) (Frankfurter, J., dissenting); accord, *United States v. Nixon,* 418 U.S. 683, 709–10 (1974).

   Trammel v. United States, 445 U.S. 40, 50–51 (1980).
6. *See* D. Louisell and C. Mueller, Federal Evidence §201, at 416, 417 (1978) and C. Wright and K. Graham, Federal Practice and Procedure §5422, at 670–72 (1980).
7. 8 J. Wigmore, Evidence §2285, at 527 (McNaughten rev. ed. 1961).
8. *See* Chapter 5.
9. Louisell, *supra* note 2, at 101; *see also Hearings on Proposed Rules of Evidence Before the Special Subcomm. on Reform of Federal Criminal Laws of the House Comm. on the Judiciary,* 93d Cong., 1st Sess. Ser. 2, at 240 (1973), *reprinted in* Black, *The Marital and Physician Privileges—A Reprint of a Letter to a Congressman,* 1975 Duke L.J. 45, 46–52 (impassioned statement that privacy concerns demand recognition of physician privilege); Krattenmaker, *Testimonial Privileges in Federal Courts: An Alternative to the Proposed Federal Rules of Evidence,* 62 Geo. L.J. 61, 85–94 (1973) (discussion of privacy as basis for testimonial privileges); Saltzburg, *Privileges and Professionals: Lawyers and Psychiatrists* 66 Va. L. Rev. 597, 605–12 (1980) (discussing privacy as opposed to utility as basis for attorney-client privilege).
10. *See* C. Wright and K. Graham, *supra* note 6, at 671.
11. C. Dewitt, Privileged Communications Between Physician and Patient 27 (1958) (footnotes omitted). This argument was first made in the American Medical Association's 1847 Code of Ethics. C. Leake, Percival's Medical Ethics 219–220 (1927). *See* Chapter 2.
12. The nature of contemporary medicine with third party reimbursement and participation of specialists and allied health professionals belies any reasonable

expectation that confidentiality exists in medicine. Siegler, *Confidentiality in Medicine—A Decrepit Concept*, 307 N. Eng. J. Med. 1518 (1982).

13. *See* 8 J. Wigmore, *supra* note 7 §2380a, at 828; Chafee, *Privileged Communications: Is Justice Served or Obstructed by Closing the Doctor's Mouth on the Witness Stand?*, 52 Yale L.J. 607, 609 (1943); Ladd, *A Modern Code of Evidence*, 27 Iowa 213, 224–25 (1942); Long, *The Physician-Patient Privilege Statutes Obstruct Justice*, 25 Ins. Co. J. 224, 224–25 (1958); Morgan, *Suggested Remedies for Obstructions to Expert Testimony by Rules of Evidence*, 10 U. Chi. L. Rev. 285, 290 (1944); Purrington, *An Abused Privilege*, 7 Col. L. Rev. 388, 396 (1906).
14. E.g., Guttmacher & Weihofen, *Privileged Communications Between Psychiatrist and Patient*, 28 Ind. L.J. 32 (1952); Louisell & Sinclair, *The Supreme Court of California, 1969–70—Foreword: Reflections on the Law of Privileged Communications—The Psychotherapist-Patient Privilege in Perspective*, 59 Calif. L. Rev. 30 (1971), Slovenko, *Psychiatry and a Second Look at the Medical Privilege*, 6 Wayne L. Rev. 175 (1960).
15. Gardner, *A Re-Evaluation of the Attorney-Client Privilege*, 8 Vill. L. Rev. 447, 481 (1963). An eloquent and empassioned plea utilizing this theory in support of a physician-patient privilege in the Federal Rules of Evidence was given by Professor Charles Black of the Yale Law School.

> Hardly less grave is the invasion of central human privacy involved in the root-and-branch abolition of the physician-patient privilege. The question here is not only whether people might be discouraged from making full communication to physicians, though it seems flatly impossible that this would not sometimes happen—a consideration which would in itself be enough to make incomprehensible the absolute subordination of this privacy interest to any trivial interest arising in litigation. But evaluation of a rule like this entails not only a guess as to what conduct it will motivate, but also an estimate of its intrinsic decency. All of us would consider it indecent for a doctor, in the course, say, of a television interview, or even in a textbook, to tell all he knows, naming names, about patients who have been treated by him. Why does this judgment of decency altogether vanish from sight, sink to absolute zero, as soon as somebody files any kind of a nondemurrable complaint in a federal court? Here, again, can a rule be a good one when the ethical doctor must violate it, or hedge, or evade?
>
> In *Rochin v. California*, 342 U.S. 165 (1952), the late Mr. Justice Frankfurter, for the Court, condemned as utterly indecent the forced pumping of a man's stomach to get criminal evidence. Does not the forced revealing of every medical and personal fact, stomach contents and all, learned by the doctor of a person not even suspected of anything, just to serve the convenience of any litigant, partake at least a little of the same indecency? Do not these and many other considerations lead to the discernment of constitutional as well as of policy issues here? If so, then the same remarks as those made above apply to the posture in which those constitutional issues are put by the promulgation of these Rules.

Black, *supra* note 9, at 49–51.

16. Louisell, *supra* note 6, at 110–11.
17. A. Westin, Privacy and Freedom 32 (1967). Westin argues that in the absence of "personal autonomy, emotional release, self-evaluation, and limited and protected communication," each of which requires privacy, democracy cannot exist. *Id.* at

32, 33–39; *see also* S. Bok, Secrets 26–28 (1982) (in-depth work exploring the ethics of secrecy); Fried, *Privacy,* 77 Yale L.J. 475 (1968) (discussion of privacy as an aspect of social order). Not all students of privacy agree, however, that it is essential to a healthy individual or democratic society. Critics point to primitive societies in which little or no privacy exists, yet individuals are emotionally healthy and the society democratic. Illustrative of these societies are the Samoans studied by Margaret Mead who have no privacy for sleeping, dressing, bathing, excretory functions, birth, or death. M. Mead, Coming of Age in Samoa 20 (1928). *See also* Bettelheim, *The Right to Privacy is a Myth,* Sat. Evening Post, July 27, 1968 at 8 (discussion of positive aspects of lack of privacy). The notion that privacy is required for a healthy democratic society is undercut somewhat by experience closer to home. Privacy in our own society has not been physically possible until relatively recently. Ironically, the technological advances that have made privacy possible have brought new threats to privacy as well. Ruebhausen & Brim, *Privacy and Behavioral Research,* 65 Colum. L. Rev. 1184, 1185 (1965).

Nevertheless, although physical privacy such as a room of one's own has not been possible until relatively recently, most vertebrates and many behaviorally advanced invertebrates observe well-defined social spacing rules that, in part, define the compromise between attraction and repulsion of members of the same species. E. Wilson, Sociobiology: The New Synthesis 256–57 (1975).

From another perspective, an attempt to avoid disclosure is thought to imply questionable behavior, an escape from the responsibility of public action. Friedrich, *Secrecy Versus Privacy: The Democratic Dilemma,* in Nomos XIII 106–07 (1971). Avoiding criticism through secrecy prevents thorough examination of thoughts and beliefs. S. Bok, *supra* at 25. Thus, rather than encouraging careful decision-making by individuals, secrecy may encourage individuals to reach untested conclusions.

18. Radin, *The Privilege of Confidential Communication Between Lawyer and Client,* 16 Calif. 487, 488 (1928).
19. *Id.* at 488–89. Originally only testimony of a slave against his master was excluded. W. Buckland, The Roman Law of Slavery 88 (reprinted 1908 and 1969). By the third century A.D., such testimony was excluded whether offered for or against the master. Exceptions were made in certain cases such as corruption of vestal virgins, adultery, and coinage offenses. *Id.* at 89–90.
20. Radin, *supra* note 18, at 488.
21. Roman law excluded the parties to a case from testifying as another aspect of the rules of incompetence. W. Buckland, A Textbook of Roman Law 637 (3d ed. 1963).
22. S. Greenleaf, A Treatise on the Law of Evidence § 247, at 289 n. 1 (13th ed. 1876).
23. Canon law developed as the exclusive law governing disputes among members of the early Christian church, although governmental recognition did not occur until the ninth century. G.D. Espinay, *De L'Influence Du Droit Canonique sur le Development De La Procedure Civile Et Criminelle* in Revue Historique De Droit Francais et Etranger, Tome II 503–505 (1st Serie 1856). Canon law fostered the

development of privileges through the use of an adversary system and a requirement that judgments be based on legally admissible evidence.

24. W. Tieman, The Right to Silence: Privileged Communication and the Pastor 30–31 (1964). *See also* 1 H. Lea, A History of Auricular Confession and Indulgences in the Latin Church 415–17 (1896).
25. H. Lea, *supra* note 24, at 415; R. Naz, Traite de Droit Canonique, Tome II, Livre III, Des Sacraments, Canons 726-153 (2d ed. Letouzey, Paris 1956).
26. Armenian and Syrian Canons in the sixth century A.D. provided for dismissal of priests breaching the seal of confession. *Canon 18 of Verses II of Achtarak,* 548–557 A.D. in Disciplinia Antiochena Antica 213 (P. Hindo ed. Sira, Vatican, 1941). Canon 22, which also provided for dismissal, was incorporated into the Canon Law Compilation of Anselm of Lucca (11th Century) and later into the Decree of Gratiam, Gratiam, Dist. VI, *De Paenit.,* C2. To this penalty, life imprisonment in a convent was added by the Council of Lateran of 1215. *Decr.,* I.V., T. XXXVIII, C-12.

    Canons 889, 890, and 2369 of the Canon Law Code of 1917 which flow from the Council of Lateran, are the present day Church law applicable to this subject. Canon 889 prohibits any breach of the seal of confession. Canon 890 prohibits the priest from using knowledge acquired at confession even absent disclosure of the secret itself. Canon 2369 imposes criminal sanctions and excommunication for violation of Canon 889. R. Naz, Traite de Droit Canonique, Tome IV, Des Delits et Des Peines, 777–78 (2nd ed. Letouzey, Paris (1954)).
27. Lea, *supra* note 24, at 455 (footnote omitted). This incident may be one of the first reported instances of the exclusionary rule.
28. C. Pen Annot. art. 378, Tome I, Livre III (annotated by E. Garon, Sirey, Paris [1901–1906]).
29. *See* Nov. 30, 1810, Cass. Crim. 1re, Fr., 1791–1830 S. Jur. I.
30. J. Thayer, *supra* note 4, at 16.
31. 8 J. Wigmore, *supra* note 7, § 2190, at 62. *See* J. Thayer, *supra* note 4, at 47–48, 90–93.
32. 8 J. Wigmore, *supra* note 7, § 2190, at 63–64; J. Thayer, *supra* note 4, at 126–29.
33. J. Thayer, *supra* note 4, at 129.
34. 8 J. Wigmore, *supra* note 7, §2190, at 65.
35. *Id.* § 2290, at 542–43. In Medieval England prior to the reign of Henry VIII, the law of the Church, then the Roman Church, and the law of England were so intertwined that the seal of the confession functioned as a priest-penitant privilege. Hogan, *A Modern Problem on the Privilege of the Confessional,* 6 Loyola L. Rev. 1, 8 (1951). Following Henry VIII's break with the Roman church a priest-penitant privilege was rejected by English courts and contemporary sources now typically state that the common law did not recognize a priest-penitant privilege. *Id.* at 2, 13.
36. 8 J. Wigmore, *supra* note 7, §2290, at 542 n. 1. Wigmore cited and analyzed the cases as follows:

> Berd v. Lovelace, Cary 88, 21 Eng. Rep. 33 (Ch. 1577) (solicitor exempted from examination touching the cause); Dennis v. Codrington, Cary 113, 21 Eng. Rep. 53

(Ch. 1580) (on a motion to examine one Oldsworth, "touching a matter in variance, wherein he hath been of Counsel, it is ordered he shall not be compelled by subpoena or otherwise to be examined upon any matter concerning the same, wherein he the said Mr. Oldsworth was of counsel, either by the indifferent choice of both parties or with either of them by reason of any annuity or fee"); Kelway v. Kelway, Cary 127, 21 Eng. Rep. 47 (Ch. 1580) (solicitor of plaintiff to be examined for defendant, "upon any interrogatory which shall not be touching the secrecy of the title or of any other matter which he knoweth as solicitor only"); Onbie's Case, March N. C. 83, pl. 136, 82 Eng. Rep. 422 (K.B. 1642) ("a lawyer who was of counsel may be examined upon oath as to the matter of agreement, not to the validity of an assurance, or to matter of counsel"); Roll, C.J., in Waldron v. Ward, Sty. 449, 82 Eng. Rep. 853 (K.B. 1654) ("He is not bound to make answer for things which may disclose the secrets of his client's cause"); Sparke v. Middleton, 1 Kebl. 505, 83 Eng. Rep. 1079 (K.B. 1664) (counsel required in testifying to tell only "such things as he either knew before he was of counsel or that came to his knowledge since by other persons"); Legard v. Foot, Rep. t. Finch 82, 23 Eng. Rep. 44 (Ch. 1673) (attorney privileged); Anonymous, Skin. 404, 90 Eng. Rep. 179 (K.B. 1693) (counsel privileged).

37. *See* e.g. E. Cleary, McCormick on Evidence §87, at 204 n. 2 (3d ed. Lawyers ed. 1984); J. Prince, Richardson on Evidence § 426, at 440 (9th ed. 1964). Professor Hazard questions whether acceptance of the attorney client privilege was firmly rooted as early as Wigmore suggests. Hazard, *An Historical Perspective on the Attorney-Client Privilege,* 77 Cal. L. Rev. 1061, 1070 (1978). According to Hazard's analysis of the early cases, recognition of the attorney-client privilege was at first viewed with much skepticism, only hesitantly accepted until the nineteenth century, and thereafter subject to exceptions for crimes and wrongdoing by the client.
38. F. W. Maitland, Constitutional History of England 5 (1926).
39. 3 W. Holdsworth, History of English Law 491 (5th ed. 1942).
40. J. Scott, Law, The State and the International Community 257 (1939). Scott defines *aequitas* as essentially the same as the Law of Nature.
41. 3 W. Holdsworth, *supra* note 39, at 491.
42. W. Windeyer, Lectures in Legal History 182–83 (2d ed. 1949).
43. Cary, 88, 21 Eng. Rep. 33 (Ch. 1577).
44. 8. J. Wigmore, *supra* note 7, §2290, at 543; 9 W. Holdsworth, History of the English Law 202 (3d ed. 1944).
45. Rex v. Duchess of Kingston, 20 How. St. Tr. 355, 572–73 (1776).
46. *Id.* at 572.
47. *Id.* at 573 (footnotes omitted). It is noteworthy that even if a physician-patient privilege had been recognized in this case, these communications might not have come within its protection. The privilege, when recognized, protects only information reasonably necessary to secure medical care. Hawkin's testimony related to delivering a child of the Duchess. *Id.* at 577. The Duchess's disclosure of the child's father may not fall within this requirement.
48. Klein, *The History of Medicine in Tudor Times: An Histographical Survey,* 33 The Historian 365, 374 (1971).
49. L. Zimmerman & I. Veith, Great Ideas in the History of Surgery 258 (1961).

50. F. Birkenhead, Famous Trials of History 66, 71, 95–99 (1926). There is evidence that medical malpractice cases were litigated in English courts at least as early as the fourteenth century. Post, *Doctor Versus Patient: Two Fourteenth Century Lawsuits,* 16 Med. Hist. 296, 296–300 (1972).
51. Geis and Bunn, *Sir Thomas Browne and Witchcraft: A Cautionary Tale for Contemporary Law and Psychiatry,* 41 Int'l J. L & Psych. 1, 2 (1981).
52. *Id.* at 3.
53. *Id.* at 2.
54. Rex. V. Duchess of Kingston, 20 How. St. Tr. 355 (1776). The earlier use of medical testimony is consistent with the experience of Roman law in which medical testimony, although not always physician testimony, was frequently received. Amundsen and Ferngren, *The Role of Physicians in Roman Law,* 58 Bull. Hist. Med. 39, 39–56 (1979).
55. Klein, *supra* note 48, at 375–77.
56. 19 How. St. Tr. 886 (1760).
57. *Id.* at 912–919.
58. W. Blackstone, Commentaries on the Laws of England 370 (1768). Blackstone states:

> All witnesses, that have the use of their reason, are to be received and examined, except such as are *infamous,* or such as are *interested* in the event of the cause. All others are *competent* witnesses; though the jury from other circumstances will judge of their *credibility.* Infamous persons are such as may be challenged as jurors, *proper delictum;* and therefore never shall be admitted to give evidence to inform that jury, with whom they were too scandalous to associate. Interested witnesses may be examined upon a *voir dire,* if suspected to be secretly concerned in the event; or their interest may be proved in court. Which last is the only method of supporting an objection to the former class; for no man is to be examined to prove his own infamy. And no counsel, attorney, or other person, intrusted with the secrets of the cause by the party himself, shall be compelled, or perhaps allowed, to give evidence of such conversation or matters of privacy, as came to his knowledge by virtue of such trust and confidence: but he may be examined as to mere matters of fact, as the execution of a deed or the like, which might have come to his knowledge without being intrusted in the cause.

59. 8 J. Wigmore, *supra* note 7, §2286, at 531.
60. *See* Wheeler v. LeMarchant, 17 Ch. D. 675, 681 (1881). A contemporary analysis of the early cases sums up their approach:

> And Lord *Brougham* in *Greenhough v. Gaskell* gives as the reason for the privilege of legal advisers that it is out of regard to the interests of justice which cannot be upholden, and to the administration of justice which cannot go on, without the aid of men skilled in jurisprudence, in the practice of the courts, and in those matters affecting rights and obligations which form the subject of all judicial proceedings. If the privilege did not exist at all, everyone would be thrown upon his own legal resources: deprived of all professional assistance, a man would not venture to consult any skillful person, or would only dare to tell his counselor half his case.

> Having regard to these considerations it is clear why the privilege, so called, is not extended to medical advisers. They have nothing to do as such with the administration of justice. The reason of the privilege in relations to legal advisors does not extend to them. It is not absolutely necessary in the interests of justice that inviolable secrecy should attach to all transactions between a man and his medical advisers. The reason for the obligation of honour on the part of medical advisers is not to enable the patient or party by whom they are consulted to obtain justice according to law, but enable him to preserve that privacy in personal matters which every man is lawfully entitled to maintain.

Professional Confidences of Medical Men, 64 Justice of the Peace 241, 242 (1900).

61. Wheeler v. LeMarchant, 17 Ch. D. 675, 681 (1881).
62. R. Cross, Evidence 258 (4th ed. 1974); Brooke, *Medicine, Pharmacy, Drugs and Medicinal Products,* Halsbury's Laws of England, ¶ 9 (Lord Hailsham ed. 1980).
63. Law Reform Committee (London), Privilege in Civil Proceedings 20–22 (Sixteenth Report 1967). Relevant portions of their report are set forth below:

> This is another confidential relationship to which no absolute privilege attaches but which, in practice, causes little difficulty. The relationship of doctor and patient enables the doctor to obtain information of two different kinds, i.e., information resulting from his clinical observation of the patient (e.g. symptoms of veneral disease) and information communicated by the patient to the doctor for the purpose of enabling him to diagnose and prescribe. The justification for treating the first kind of information as confidential is that it improves the health of the nation by encouraging persons to seek medical advice and treatment. The justification for treating the second kind of information as confidential is that candour on the part of the patient is essential in order to determine the appropriate treatment for him. But in the great majority of civil cases in which doctors are called as witnesses they are called by the patient himself to give evidence of fact or opinion as to the patient's condition . . .
>
> • • •
>
> Personal injury cases are the commonest of those in which doctors are called as witnesses; but there may be others in which justice cannot be done without a doctor's disclosing information which he has obtained in the course of the doctor-patient relationship. Medical negligence cases, issues as to the sanity or testamentary capacity of the patient and statements made to obtain life insurance are examples. It is said, no doubt with justification, that successful psychiatric treatment is dependent upon the utmost candour and confidence between doctor and patient and that psychiatrists are the recipients of a wide variety of confidences which might be relevant as admissions upon issues other than the health of the patient. But we find it difficult to envisage situations which are not fanciful in which a psychiatrist is likely to be called as a witness except on an issue as to the mental or emotional state of a patient; and, since a psychiatric diagnosis depends largely upon what the patient has told the psychiatrist, we find it impracticable to draw any line *a priori* between communications by the patient which ought to be disclosed to enable the accuracy of the diagnosis to be tested and those which it is unnecessary to disclose for this purpose.
>
> These considerations have driven us to the conclusion that, where a doctor is called, whether by the patient himself or by some other party, to give evidence

upon an issue as to the mental or physical condition of one of his patients, it is impracticable to define in a statute the circumstances in which he should be permitted to refuse to answer questions upon information obtained from the patient as his medical adviser unless the patient consents to his doing so. The propriety of allowing him to refuse must depend upon all the circumstances of the case and is, we think, best left, as at present, to the judge. The way in which judges have exercised that discretion in the past in civil cases has given little ground for complaint from the medical profession and we think that they can be relied on in the future to hold the balance fairly between the Hippocratic oath and the witness's oath to tell the whole truth....

* * *

In arriving at the conclusion that no statutory privilege should be conferred on communications made either to priests or doctors, we have been concerned to avoid making recommendations inconsistent with such views as may be expressed by the Criminal Law Revision Committee. It is in criminal, rather than in civil, proceedings that there is likely to arise any question of a priest or doctor being compelled to reveal communications made to him in confidence by a penitent or patient. For the reasons we have given, the issue is one of little practical importance in civil proceedings, but it would be anomalous, and would imply a false set of values, if we were to rate the secrecy of the confessional or the inviolability of the Hippocratic oath as more important than the ascertainment of the truth about a crime, but not as important as the ascertainment of the truth about a private wrong to an individual. However, we have been informed that, after a thorough examination of these questions, the Criminal Law Revision Committee does not propose to recommend any change in the existing law. In this respect, our own conclusions do not differ from theirs.

64. *See* Mole v. Mole, (1950) 2 All. E.R. 328, 329; McTaggart v. McTaggart, (1948) 2 All E.R. 754, 755.
65. N.Y. Rev. Stat. 1829 II, 406, Part III, Title 3, Ch. VII, Art. VIII § 79. The original statute provided:

    No person duly authorized to practice physic or surgery, shall be compelled to disclose any information which he may have acquired in attending any patient, in professional character, and which information was necessary to enable him to prescribe for such patient as a physician, or to do any act for him, as a surgeon.

66. *Extracts from the Original Reports of the Revisers,* Revised Statutes of the State of New York (1836).
67. 100 Eng. Rep. 1283, 1287 (K.B. 1792).
68. *Id.* at 1287 (footnote omitted).
69. Transactions of the Medical Society of the State of New York 1807–31, 230, 242 (1868).
70. C. Dewitt, *supra* note 11.
71. Group for the Advancement of Psychiatry, Report No. 45, *Confidentiality and Privileged Communications in the Practice of Psychiatry* (Report No. 45, 1960).
72. Shuman and Weiner, *supra* note 3, at 907–911.
73. New Zealand Evidence Act 1908, §8 *reprinted in part in* Finlay, *Confidentiality of Medical Disclosures—Looking Ahead,* 1975 New Zealand L.J. 80, 81.

74. Victoria Evidence Act 1958 (Vic.) S. 28 (as amended by Act 7418 [1966]).
75. Section 49 of the Israel Evidence Ordinance.
76. Tasmania Evidence Act of 1910, 96, 2 Tas. St.
77. Bernfeld, *Medical Secrecy,* 3 Cambrian L. Rev. 11, 14 (1972).
78. *Id.*
79. Dickens, *Legal Protection of Psychiatric Confidentiality,* 1 Int'l J.L. & Psychiatry 255, 260 (1978). Although common law Canada has refused any formal recognition of a physician-patient privilege, caselaw indicates some support for a marital therapist privilege. *See, e.g.,* Dembie v. Dembie, 21 R.F.L. 46 (Ont. Sup. Ct. 1976).
80. Que. Rev. Stat. ch. M-9, §42 (1977). *See* Tollefson, *Privileged Communications in Canada (Common Law Provinces),* 4 Int'l Symp. on Comp. L. 32, 44–45 (1967).
81. Bernfeld, *supra* note 77, at 14.
82. Zeffertt, *Confidentiality and the Courts,* 91 S. African L.J. 432, 434–35 (1974).
83. *Supra* note 13.
84. *Supra* note 14.
85. *See* Chapter 2.
86. Ill. Rev. Stat. ch. 51, §5.2 (1972).
87. San Francisco v. Superior Court, 37 Cal.2d 227, 231 P.2d 26 (1951).
88. Tex. R. Evid. 509(d) (2).
89. Tex. R. Crim. Evid. 509.
90. State v. Dayton Press, 11 Ohio St. 3d 66, 463 N.E.2d 1243 (1984).
91. Gaynier v. Johnson, 673 S.W.2d 899 (Tex. App.—Dallas 1984, no writ).
92. Tex. R. Evid. 509(d) (4).
93. Tex. R. Evid. 509 (d) (6).
94. Shuman, Psychiatric and Psychological Evidence §10.05 (1986).
95. Digest, L 25, D. de Testibus, 22, 5 cited in A. Allard, Histoire de la Justice Criminelle § 137, 253–55 (Gand 1868), "(N)e patroni in causa cui patrocinium praestiterunt, testimonium dicant." *Id.* at 253. The attorney-client and priest-penitent professional secret in French law have been similarly traced.
96. M. Giraud, Essai sur L'Histoire du Droit Francais au Moyen Age, Tome I, 15–35 (Paris 1846).
97. *Id.* at 35–44.
98. A. Esmain, Histoire de la Procédure Criminelle en France 46–47 (Paris 1882).
99. G. Le Bras, *L'Englise Medievale au Service du Droit Romain,* in Revue Historique de Droit Francais et Etranger, Tome XLIV, 195 (4th Serie 1966). A letter from Pope John VIII in 814 A.D. hints that Roman law soon became one of the sources of canon law. "Venerandae Romanae Leges Divinitum per ora Principum Promulgatae," Decret C., 16, Q. 3C. 17.
100. Decretum Gratiani, C.4, Q.2, C3 (Witnesses).
101. G. Le Bras, *supra* note 99, at 195. This also gave formal recognition to the absoluteness of the seal of confession.
102. *See* A. Allard, *supra* note 95, §137, at 253–55; G. Le Bras, *supra* note 99, at 197–200.
103. *Médecine,* Dictionnaire Encyclopédique Quillet 4154 (Paris 1975).

104. *Art. 19 Appendicis ad Reformationem ein Facultatis Medicinae,* in Domat, Les Lois Civiles, Le Droit Public, Tome I, Livre 2, at 129, XIII (1777).
105. Guyot, Repertoire de Jurisprudence, Tome XI, 438–41 (Paris 1785).
106. E. Glasson, Histoire du Droit et des Institutions de la France, Tome VI, 542 (Paris 1895).
107. 1858 D. Jur. I 476.
108. Papon. Liv. 24, Tit. 7.
109. Allard, *supra* note 95, §137, at 253–54.
110. Menochius, Praes, Lib. 1, Q89.
111. May 1, 1899, Cass. civ., Fr., 1901 S. Jur. I, 162 u. §1.
112. "Physicians, Surgeons and Pharmacists are forbidden to declare the secret ailments of those whom they try to heal." Ferriere, Dictionnaire de Droit et Pratique, 93 (Paris 1769).
113. May 1, 1899, Cass. civ., Fr., 1901 S. Jur. I, 161.
114. *Id.*
115. *Id.* French case law dating from the sixteenth century recognized a duty of confidentiality upon the physician. 1854 D. Jur. I 27 §82, §83. The moral duty of the Hippocratic Oath was transfered into a legal duty for which the patient might bring action for damages when the disclosure was malicious. 1858 D. Jur. I, 476–77. For example, in 1599 the Chambre de la Tournelle rendered a judgment against a pharmacist who had disclosed a patient's loathesome disease because of the patient's default in paying the bill. *Id.* The duty not to disclose is evidenced in part by a 1666 edict that required physicians to reveal to municipal authorities treatment given to injured patients so that the authorities could track down criminal activities. *Id.*, at 476, §4. Although unenforced due to its unpopularity, the edict is a response to the duty of secrecy.
116. C. Pen. Annot. art. 139.
117. Serpillan, Code Criminel, 1se partie, 447 (Lyon 1767).
118. 1858 D. Jur. I, 477. Originally article 378 was categorized as a defamatory crime and only slanderous disclosures punishable. Thus, for example, a physician who attended a birth and thereby discovered evidence of an earlier abortion was liable for disclosure only if the patient enjoyed a good reputation. This interpretation of the professional secret codified in Article 378 was abandoned toward the second half of the nineteenth century. *Id.* at 477–78.

    Article 378 did not work a radical change in existing law, but was instead built upon existing law. Perraud-Charmantier, Le Secret Professional, Introduction 35–39, 55–64. (Parts 1926).
119. Locre, La Legislation Civile, Commerciale et Criminelle de la France, Tome XV, Code Civil, Livre III, 445.
120. R. Floriot et R. Courbaldieu, Le Secret Professionnel 17–18 (1973).
121. *Id.* at 18.
122. *Id.* at 42–43.
123. *Id.* at 7.
124. *Id.* at 72.
125. *Id.* at 13, 28.

126. *Id.*
127. Nerson, *Journal des Tribunaux 175* (1959), quoted in Privacy and Human Rights 59 (A. Robertson ed. 1973).
128. J. B. de la Gressaye, Secret Professionnel, Repertoire de Droit Penal et de Procedure Penale, Tome IV (Dalloz, Paris 1977).
129. *Id.*
130. D. Thouveuin, Le Secret Medical et L'Information du Malache 98 (1982).
131. Honorat et Melennec, *Vers Une Relativisation du Secret Medical,* 1979 J.C.P. I. No. 2936, ¶ 1.
132. *Id.* No. 2936 at 18–20. A 1966 decision of the French Cour de Cassation is illustrative. Dame Bordier, 22 Decembre 1966 Cass., crim. 1967 J.L.P. II No. 15126. The defendant was charged with murdering her lover and cutting his body into little pieces. She attempted to call her personal physician but was refused the opportunity based upon the absolute nature of the professional secret. Over a dissenting opinion, the majority of the court reasoned that patient trust requires that the secret be absolute and beyond the capacity of the patient, physician or judge to waive.

    A Canadian law Professor, Jack London, described a rape trial he observed in the south of France. The defense alleged was consent. The accused sought to present the testimony of a nurse that shortly after the alleged rape contrary to the victims' testimony, the two alleged victims were "in good spirits and sound physical condition." When the nurse was informed that her testimony, even with the patient-victim's consent, would constitute a violation of professional secrecy cognizable under the criminal law, she refused to testify. The defendants were convicted. London, *Privacy in the Medical Context,* in Aspects of Privacy Law 281, 282 (D. Gibson 1980).
133. Honorat & Melennec, *supra* note 131.
134. *Id.*
135. *Id.*
136. Honorat & Melennec, *supra* note 131, ¶22.
137. Slachmuylder, *Secret professionnel et protection de la Jeunesse,* Journal des Tribunaux Oct. 7, 1967, at 529–32.
138. J. B. de la Gressaye, *supra* note 128, at 4, 5.
139. *Id.*
140. *Id.*
141. *Id.* A recent example of cognizable violation occurred in a case in which a physician consultant for an insurance company obtained access to the insured's hospital records and disclosed to the insurance company that the patient suffered from a terminal disease and had a very limited life expectancy at the time of the accident. Docteur B . . . , Mai 17, 1973 Cass., crim., 1974 J.C.P. II No. 17712. The Cour de Cassation affirmed a judgment finding that the physician violated the professional secret since he knew he was disclosing confidential information acquired in a professional capacity even though the information was obtained from a source other than the patient.
142. German Penal Code of 1871, article 300 (1961).

143. Swiss Penal Code, article 321.
144. Italian Penal Code, article 622 (1978).
145. Belgian Penal Code, article 458 (1810).
146. Decree Law 32,171, July 29, 1942, Art. 7 (Portugal).
147. Damaska, *Evidentiary Barriers to Conviction and Two Models of Criminal Procedure: A Comparative Study,* 121 U. Pa. L. Rev. 506, 507 (1973).

Chapter 5

EMPIRICAL RESEARCH

The utilitarian arguments favoring a psychotherapist-patient privilege discussed in Chapter 3 rest, in part, on the assumption that the privilege is necessary for effective therapy. Unfortunately, in most of the debates on the desirability of the privilege, anecdotal rather than well designed empirical research is advanced to support this assumption. This chapter presents empirical studies that bear on issues related to privilege. It begins with a review of the empirical literature conducted by others and concludes with the presentation of the authors' three studies.

I. Literature Review

The first group of studies discussed were not designed to test the importance of privilege, but instead to measure the importance of confidentiality in nonjudicial settings. In 1978, Singer[1] undertook a social survey of 2,084 potential respondents designed to measure the importance of confidentiality in social science research. She made absolute assurances of confidentiality to one-third, qualified assurances of confidentiality to one-third, and no mention of confidentiality to the remaining third. Her questions included sensitive issues, such as masturbation and frequency of sexual intercourse, as well as more neutral questions. She found a consistently lower, but not always statistically significant nonresponse rate on sensitive items when there was a guarantee of absolute confidentiality.

A 1977 study in Georgia by Rosen[2] sought to measure conditions affecting patients' willingness to release information. When 658 psychiatric clinic patients were told to sign forms consenting to release information about their diagnosis to the State of Georgia, all complied. When 241 patients in another clinic were given the option not to comply, 59 percent did not sign the release. In a third clinic, the compliance rate dropped to 21 percent when patients were offered a choice. The author concluded that psychiatric outpatients relinquish the privacy of their records because they think they have no choice, not because they are unconcerned.

Bernal y del Rio[3] surveyed psychoanalysts about their analysands' reactions to the government-authorized break-in and search for Daniel Ellsberg's records at psychoanalyst Lewis Fielding's office. Of those surveyed, 861 (62 percent) replied and reported on 5,074 analysands. Only 13 percent of the analysands made verbal references to the break-in. The analysts estimated that related manifest dream content occurred in another 1.5 percent and latent dream content in 2.6 percent. The author concluded found that analysands are confident about the privacy of their communications, regardless of legal or physical safeguards.

Appelbaum[4] interviewed 58 patients in a university hospital psychiatric clinic to ascertain if the absence of confidentiality would have discouraged them from seeking or freely taking part in psychiatric treatment. Nearly 80 percent had been previously hospitalized. Their age range was broad (67 years) with a mean age of 40. Most patients (85 percent) were unmarried and most were white Catholics. Twenty-five open-ended questions were used to determine how greatly patients valued confidentiality and their feelings about disclosure under varying circumstances. Only 62 percent reported they would feel negatively if their therapist revealed information about them without their consent. When asked about release of records to persons outside the clinic, three-quarters expressed negative feelings. Many of the patients were or had been embarrassed about being in therapy and four-fifths thought that others considered it something to be ashamed of. Relatively few patients (10 percent), however, had ever been concerned about their therapist disclosing about them without their permission. Only two of 58 patients wanted their records absolutely secret. Nearly half would limit disclosure to those directly concerned with their care, and 21 percent would allow release to any physician or mental health professional.

Of further interest is that all but one patient said that other people were aware of their being in therapy, and in 93 percent of the cases, the patients themselves were the source of information. More than half of the patients indicated that their therapist revealing information about them without their consent would negatively affect their relationship with the therapist.

Appelbaum noted that, as in a previous study of inpatients,[5] patients were not concerned about absolute confidentiality. Rather, they were primarily concerned that information about them be used to further their treatment and not to embarrass them or to prejudice others.

These studies speak to the importance of confidentiality in therapy. To varying degrees they suggest that patients are concerned about confidentiality. But, they do not suggest that patients consider the risk of court-ordered disclosure as a threat to confidentiality. In the second group of studies, the importance of a privilege to the therapeutic relationship was sought to be evaluated.

A survey of Massachusetts psychiatrists before their state's privilege statute was enacted, by Suarez and Balcanoff,[6] found that court-ordered disclosure of confidential information was rare. Of 487 respondents, only 28 percent said they had had at least one experience in which privilege had been a significant issue in the preceding five years. In 18 instances (eight respondents), the judge limited disclosure of the communication. Disclosure of intimate material in court was required of the psychiatrists only four other times, and therapy records were subpoenaed only five times during the five-year period. Nearly all of the forced disclosures involved child custody, an issue to which an exception to privilege is often recognized.

In a questionnaire study of psychiatrists, psychologists, marriage counselors, lawyers, judges, and lay persons conducted by the Yale Law Review in 1962, 71 percent of the lay group reported that they would be less likely to disclose themselves fully to a counselor without protection of their communication.[7] Nearly one-third (31 percent) of the lay group had sought counseling with marriage counselors, social workers, psychologists, or psychiatrists, but only nine (8.3 percent) of them were seeing a counselor regularly at the time they completed the questionnaire. Of the psychiatrists, 15 (43 percent) had been called to testify in court about patients or ex-patients. Of those called on to testify, 75 percent had done so less than ten times, but only three had ever been forced to disclose confidential information.

The professionals surveyed agreed overwhelmingly that privilege encouraged disclosure by patients and that its lack discouraged disclosure. In addition, the possibility of being called to the witness stand significantly affected the recordkeeping of psychiatrists, psychologists, and marriage counselors. Their records tended to be vague, containing little information of value for legal or treatment purposes.

A later survey by the California Law Review[8] of 179 psychologists and 1,093 psychiatrists from California followed the state's Supreme Court decision in the *Tarasoff*[9] case that held that the duty of mental health professionals may in certain instances extend to a third party endangered by their patient. Most respondents (79 percent) replied affirmatively to the question, "Once a patient is aware that you might have to discuss his case with someone else, do you think he is less likely to divulge certain information?" Moreover, only 11 percent of this group always discussed confidentiality with patients. Most discussed the limits of confidentiality only if the issue arose during treatment. Of the respondents, 24.5 percent found patients reluctant to discuss violent tendencies once told that the case might need to be discussed with someone else. Another quarter of the respondents (25.7 percent) had patients who dropped out of treatment because they feared breach of confidentiality. The number of patients lost to therapists who threatened disclosure ranged from one to 100 (median, three patients). Of the psychiatrists and psychologists whose patients left treatment, 23 percent said their patients refused further treatment, 11 percent said patients returned to therapy or were successfully referred to someone else, and 63 percent did not know what happened to their patients afterward.

This survey also revealed that California therapists had been warning endangered third parties before they had a legal duty to do so. Only 26 percent said that confidentiality should never be breached.

The only empirical research regarding the impact of privilege on the discovery of legally relevant information was a questionnaire study of 47 judges by the Yale Law Review.[7] Although 91 percent of those surveyed thought that limited privilege for lawyers was obstructive, 89 percent said that it did not significantly disrupt fact finding, and 85 percent thought that it did not need further limitation. When asked about privilege for helping professions, 62 percent of the judges favored privilege for psychiatrists, 43 percent for psychologists, and 45 percent for marriage counselors. In contrast, no judge favored privilege for real estate brokers or business associates, and only 17 percent favored privilege for accountants.

II. The Authors' Studies

The utilitarian arguments for privilege suggest the need to examine the following hypotheses:

1. Lay persons and psychotherapy patients are greatly concerned about the confidentiality of patient-psychotherapist communications.
2. Lack of privilege deters potential patients from seeking psychological or psychiatric help.
3. Lack of privilege delays help-seeking.
4. Lack of privilege impairs the quality of treatment because patients' fears of disclosure reinforce conscious and unconscious resistances.
5. Lack of privilege causes premature termination of therapy by those who are the greatest danger to themselves and society.
6. Patients are psychologically harmed if therapists disclose their confidential communications.
7. The discovery of truth at trial is hindered by privilege.

To address these issues a survey was made of lay persons, psychotherapy patients, psychiatrists, and judges. The questionnaires are presented as Tables 1–4. The authors were able to incorporate into the Texas study a major Texas health insurer's figures for psychotherapy sessions before and after the passage in 1979 of a physician-patient privilege statute. In fact, it was the passage of the Texas privilege statute that stimulated the first study, which was designed to measure the impact of that statute.

In the course of the Texas study,[10] it was discovered that only the states of South Carolina and West Virginia lacked a physician, psychiatrist, psychologist, or psychotherapist-patient privilege statute. At the conclusion of the Texas study, it was decided to contrast the Texas findings with findings from a comparable study in those states.[11] Still later, one of the authors had the opportunity to perform a similar study in Canada, contrasting the common-law province of Ontario in which no privilege exists with the civil law province of Quebec in which a professional secret comparable to a privilege exists.[12] Those studies are presented in the pages that follow.

For statistical analysis, the Student's T test for parametric data, and the Chi Square (X^2) test for nonparametric data were employed. Yates's correction for the Chi Square test was used in all four-fold tables. Fisher's Exact test was employed in four-fold tables with cells of less than 5. The median instead of the mean was employed in presenting data concerning frequency of outpatient visits, the number of times therapists had been requested to disclose in court, and the number of warnings made by therapists to endangered those parties. This was done to prevent skewing by occasional therapists who reported large numbers of disclosures. The median was also employed for other data concerning psychiatrists and judges to obtain a better impression of the model therapist or judge.

The results of the studies are presented in table form. Lay data for all studies are presented in Table 5. Patient data for all studies are presented in Table 6. Therapist data are presented in Table 7. Judicial data for each study are presented in Table 8. The insurance company study is presented in Table 9.

A. U.S. Study

1. Texas Study

Lay questionnaires were distributed at evening adult education classes at a local university. Of the 200 distributed, 121 were returned. Students were told that the questionnaire was a voluntary survey on confidentiality to be answered anonymously. Questionnaires were returned to the instructor at the end of class.

The patient questionnaire was distributed by 31 psychiatrists who agreed to give questionnaires to five patients in therapy. In this and in the following studies, psychiatrists were asked to explain that it was part of a research project, that the respondents' names would not be known to the investigators, and that patients were free not to participate.

The questionnaires were mailed anonymously by the patients to the investigators in self-addressed envelopes. Of 160 patient questionnaires, 79 (50 percent) were returned.

Therapist questionnaires were mailed to members of the North Texas Psychiatric Society, nearly all of whom practice in or near Dallas. They were asked them to complete the questionnaires and to return them anonymously by mail. Of the 186 mailed, 84 (45 percent) were returned.

The judicial questionnaires served as a guide to a group of Southern Methodist University law students, who interviewed 48 of the 56 state and federal judges in Dallas County with generally unlimited jurisdiction over civil and criminal cases.

a. Lay Study

Nearly all (93 percent) of the 121 respondents indicated that they would seek help from a psychiatrist or psychologist for a serious emotional problem. They were asked about their willingness to disclose information in therapy under three conditions: no mention of privilege (Question 2), privilege (question 6), and no privilege (Question 7). Question 6 was omitted from tabulation in this and the following studies because the results are essentially identical to Question 2. There was no significant difference in disclosure of items when there was no mention of privilege and when the condition of privilege was suggested; p values[13] ranged from .357 to .789 for all items except sexual fantasies ($p = .169$) and masturbation ($p = .066$). Willingness to disclose all items dropped significantly ($p < .001$) for all items under a no-privilege condition except for masturbation ($p = .015$), which dropped considerably at the mere mention of confidentiality. Sexual issues were the most closely guarded under all conditions. The items affected most by the no-privilege condition were driving in excess of speed limits and work failure. There was much less of a drop in willingness to disclose sexual fantasies or masturbation under the no-privilege condition because of less initial willingness to disclose this kind of information.

There was little concern about disclosure of information to insurance carriers, state agencies, or potential employers, and mild concern (22 percent) about release to a lawyer for a trial. Two thirds of the group did not know if there was a privilege statute, and one fourth knew or guessed correctly that privilege existed in Texas. The respondents assumed that privilege was less likely to apply to questions of murder or child custody than to personal injury.

b. Patient Study

All but one of the 31 psychiatrists who distributed patient questionnaires were in private practice. The median length of therapy reported by patients was three years. Their ages ranged from 17 to 84 years (median = 36), with three-quarters women, most married, and a large number (31 percent) of professionals.

Of the patient group, 73 percent thought there was no privilege statute or did not know whether one existed. Confidentiality had been a concern for 50 percent of the patients when deciding about treatment, but only 28 percent had asked their therapists about confidentiality, and only 13 percent took additional steps to ensure it. In general, patients reported relying more heavily on the psychiatrist's ethics than on a privilege statute. A few (8 percent) said that knowledge of the statute would have led to earlier treatment.

Nearly 40 percent of the respondents had withheld information from their psychiatrist. Of the items withheld, 70 percent concerned sexual acts (36 percent) and thoughts (34 percent). Thoughts of violence, including suicide, accounted for only 9 percent of items withheld. None withheld disclosing acts of violence, if any, and withholding information about possible crimes and drug use, if any was relatively rare.

Significant differences were found between the lay group and the patient group in age ($p < .0001$), marital status ($p < .001$), and occupation ($p < .002$), and in male-female ratio ($p = .049$). Although similar in age range (17 to 57 years for the lay group versus 17 to 59 years for the patient group), the mean age of the patients was 12 years greater (17 ± 9.2 years versus 25.7 ± 7.2 years).

There was no significant difference between the number of patients and lay persons who thought there was a privilege ($X^2 = .002$, 1 df, n.s.).[14] The types of information that the lay respondents said they would withhold was similar to that withheld by the patients. Lay persons were most hesitant to disclose masturbation, sexual fantasies, and other sexual acts, and least hesitant to discuss speeding, physical violence, and work failure under the privilege condition. Under the condition of no privilege, all disclosure dropped significantly ($p < .001$), but speeding and work failure became the most sensitive topics, while cheating on income tax and theft were less strongly affected. The patient group was most sensitive to disclosure of sexual issues, but disclosed more in other areas than lay persons said they would.

c. Therapist Study

The respondents' time in practice ranged from zero to 46 years (median, 11 years). The majority (55) were in full-time private practice and were almost equally divided between outpatients (28) and combined hospital/outpatient (27) practice. Respondents saw an average of 30 patients per week, and the frequency of outpatient visits ranged from one to five times per week (median, one visit per week). A variety of psychotherapeutic approaches was used. Psychoanalysis was uncommon as a treatment, and most respondents reported using psychoanalytic[15] and supportive psychotherapy.

Of the respondents, 39 (46 percent) had been requested to disclose information in court, but only one third of those requested (15 percent of the total group) actually had been required to do so. Approximately 128 requests (median, two per physician) for disclosure had been made. It was not possible to ascertain from the data the exact total number of court appearances, but it was estimated that one courtroom disclosure occured per psychiatrist per 11 years of practice.

None of the respondents knew if any of their patients had been harmed by court disclosure, but 13 of them indicated that they did not know the impact of their action. Approximately 12 patients were in therapy at the time of the disclosure. Of those, two terminated treatment prematurely, and two reported that subsequent therapy was affected. In one case, the disclosure became the focus of therapy. In the other, the level of trust changed, apparently in a negative direction.

Of the approximately 23 patients who had terminated therapy before the disclosure, five returned for further treatment with the same psychiatrist. One ex-patient brought a malpractice suit against the physician.

Of the psychiatrists, 40 (48 percent) had also warned endangered nonprofessionals such as family members. Forty-two warnings had been made in the previous year. A total of 200 warnings had been made during the cumulative careers of the respondents, a median of three warnings during a median professional lifetime of 11 years. The psychiatrists' warnings affected patient treatment in 16 cases (8 percent), with reactions varying from relief to violence. Four patients terminated therapy prematurely.

Most psychiatrists (86 percent) discussed patients with colleagues. Most (85 percent) had initially raised the question of confidentiality at some time, but only 18 percent did so routinely. The largest group did so only when legal problems or a courtroom appearance seemed likely (18 percent); when reassuring a patient, often a child or adolescent, who raised the issue (9 percent); or, when there was danger to the patient or others (8 percent).

When asked by patients if communications were held in strict confidence, 45 percent of the respondents told them that confidentiality would be maintained unless patients were dangerous to themselves, 21 percent said it would be upheld unless a court ordered disclosure, and 11 percent said that confidentiality was absolute. Only one therapist wrote that he responded by asking, "Why do you ask?"

Most patients (79 percent) accepted the limits of confidentiality well. A few became defensive, hesitant, or angry, and one left therapy. One psychiatrist said that he thought patients did not freely confide their deepest urges or fantasies because of limited privilege.

More than half (55 percent) of the respondents did not know of the Texas privilege statute, but few (22 percent) thought that the present legal status of confidentiality in Texas limited patients' disclosures.

Issues related to confidentiality and disclosure of information had a small but definite effect on therapy. When psychiatrists warned or threatened to warn third parties of possible danger, patients usually responded positively, but some terminated therapy. For a few, disclosure sipnificantly altered therapy. No psychiatrist could document psychological harm as a result of a courtroom disclosure, but many were no longer treating particular patients when called to testify about them. Two of the 21 patients in therapy at the time the psychiatrist testified dropped out of treatment, but some returned later to the same physician to continue therapy.

d. Judicial Study

Forty-eight judges were interviewed. Of the eight who dealt with domestic relations cases, all but one had had the admissibility of a confidential communication between a psychotherapist and patient arise in court. The issue was rare for four of the eight judges (about one case per year) and considerably more frequent for the other three (five, ten, and 50 cases per year). Before enactment of the privilege statute, these judges admitted relevant therapist-patient communications into evidence, and only one imposed a higher threshhold of relevance than for other types of communication. Although most judges said that the therapist-patient communications were important to the case, four said they were never necessary for accurate resolution of contested cases; three said they were.

Two judges who dealt with probate/mental health cases reported that their experience was almost exclusively with court ordered psychiatric examinations to determine the need for involuntary hospitalization.

Of the 17 judges who handled other types of civil cases, seven had faced issues of confidentiality, which had arisen ten or less times for each. Two judges with 18 years' experience had never encountered the issue. Those judges who had encountered the issue indicated that before enactment of the privilege statute, they had admitted relevant confidential patient-therapist communications into evidence. Only one judge indicated imposing a higher standard of relevance for these communications before the statute's enactment or a requirement that this information first be sought from a nonconfidential source.

Only five of the 21 judges who heard criminal cases reported experience with cases that raised the question of admissibility of communication between a patient and psychiatrist or psychologist. Most of this experience involved court-ordered examinations for competence to stand trial.

In general, judges did not think that disclosure of therapist-patient communications was sought to harass litigants or to promote settlement. The psychiatric or psychological testimony at issue was usually deemed important to the case and unavailable from other sources. Most judges thought the information thus derived was necessary for accurate resolution of contested factual issues, but a few did not.

The only category of cases in which privilege was a frequent issue was domestic relations, dealings with child custody, visitation rights, and termination of parental rights.

e. Insurance Study

If the existence of a psychotherapist-patient privilege removes disincentives to seeking psychotherapy, there should be an increase in the number of persons in psychotherapeutic treatment coincidental with a privilege's enactment. It seemed likely that an increase in the number of psychotherapy patients would result in an increased number of insurance claims for psychotherapeutic treatment.

To test these hypotheses, information was obtained from Blue Cross/Blue Shield of Texas for the years 1976 through 1980. A 95 percent confidence interval was constructed (i.e., odds of 1:20 for a number being outside that range by chance) for the years 1976–1979 for initial psychiatric interviews, one-hour psychotherapy, half-hour psychotherapy, 45-minute psychotherapy, group psychotherapy, and total patient visits.

The 1980 figure for initial psychiatric interviews was contained within a 95 percent confidence interval for the 1976–1979 figures (mean = 9,948; S.D.[16] = 1.683). The number of 1980 visits for one-hour psychotherapy was contained within a 95 percent confidence interval for the 1976–1979 figures (mean = 10,873; S.D. = 5,193). The same was true for half-hour psychotherapy (1976–1979 mean = 120,107; S.D. = 25,412). There was an increase beyond the 95 percent confidence interval for 45-minute psychotherapy (1976–1979 mean = 6,888; S.D. = 2,119) and when the figures for total patient visits was examined, the number for 1980 was contained within the 95 percent confidence interval for the years 1976–1979 (mean = 184,828; S.D. = 7,527). During the period of time examined, there was no overall change in the scope of insurance coverage. There was, however, a decline in Blue Cross/Blue Shield enrollment of 12 percent from 1,484,161 in 1976 to 1,307,778 in 1980. That decrease was paralleled by a 5 percent decrease in initial psychiatric interviews (X^2 = .08, 1 df, n.s.), the service that would have expected to increase most had there been a significant rise in utilization for the year.

Therefore, the enactment of the privilege statute had no measurable impact on insurance-financed psychotherapy. The changes in the type of psychotherapy related to changes in the delivery patterns of psychotherapeutic services rather than increased usage. It is conceivable, however, that increased usage might not be indicated by insurance company records. Increased confidence that therapists would not be forced to disclose might not be accompanied by decreased concern about having a record of receiving psychiatric services and there being a need for therapists to submit a psychiatric diagnosis to be paid.

2. South Carolina/West Virginia Study

This study was conducted in the only two states then lacking either a physician, psychiatrist, psychologist, or psychotherapist-patient privilege. Lay persons were queried by means of questionnaires distributed in undergraduate psychology courses at the University of West Virginia. Approximately 150 were distributed; 103 (69 percent were returned). The authors were unable to secure the cooperation of a South Carolina psychologist to distribute our questionnaires in a similar setting.

Therapists were queried by means of questionnaires mailed to all 248 members of the South Carolina and West Virginia Psychiatric Societies. Forty-eight (19 percent) were returned. Stamped, self-addressed envelopes were included for return of the questionnaires to the authors.

The investigators also included sample patient questionnaires with the therapist questionnaires. Psychiatrists who were willing to distribute patient questionnaires were asked to indicate by returning a form in a self-addressed stamped envelope. Each of the 19 psychiatrists who volunteered to distribute questionnaires was mailed sets of five questionnaires and stamped, self-addressed return envelopes. Forty-one (43 percent) were returned.

Judges were queried by mail and responded anonymously.

a. Lay Study

Almost all (92.5 percent) of the 103 respondents indicated that they would seek help from a psychiatrist or psychologist for a serious emotional problem. They were asked their willingness to disclose under the conditions of no mention of privilege, privilege, and no privilege. There was no significant difference in disclosure of topics between the condition of no mention of privilege and privilege ($X^2 = .07$, 1 df, n.s.), but a significant difference occurred between the privilege and no-privilege conditions ($X^2 = 9.83$, 1 df, $p < .01$). The items affected most by the no-privilege condition were stealing and theft. Masturbation showed little change because it was the most sensitive topic.

There was little concern about disclosure to insurance carriers, state agencies, and potential employers, and mild concern (14 percent) about disclosure in a trial. Half the group did not know if there was a privilege and only 8 percent knew or guessed correctly that there was no privilege. Respondents assumed that if a privilege existed it applied more to murder or compensation issues than to child custody.

b. Therapist Study

The therapist questionnaire for the South Carolina/West Virginia study was mailed to all 248 members of the South Carolina and West Virginia Psychiatric Societies. There were 48 questionnaires returned, a return rate of 19 percent. Of the South Carolina/West Virginia psychiatrists who responded, nearly half (48 percent) practiced in counties of less than 100,000 population.

The median age of the psychiatrists was 44 years and the median length of practice was 11 years. The male-female ratio was 12:1. Relatively few (8 per cent) were in full-time outpatient practice.

Psychoanalysis was employed rarely in this sample (2 percent of therapists). Psychoanalytic psychotherapy was employed by 58 percent of therapists. Supportive psychotherapy, behavior therapy, cognitive therapy, and hypnosis were all frequently employed in South Carolina/West Virginia. The average number of patients seen per week was 41, the median frequency of outpatient visits was once a week.

Most psychiatrists (62 percent) had been requested to disclose confidential patient communications in court. Forty-three percent of those requested, 27 percent of the entire group of 48, were ultimately required to disclose those communications. The median number of requests for disclosure per professional lifetime was two. Twenty-three percent of the South Carolina/West Virginia psychiatrists who had testified in court thought that damage had been done to their patients, including loss of self-esteem and depression. Premature termination of treatment resulting from the courtroom disclosure was reported by 15 percent and 13 percent of South Carolina/West Virginia psychiatrists found therapy adversely affected. Most patients (69 percent) returned to therapy after their therapist's courtroom disclosure.

About half the South Carolina/West Virginia psychiatrists had warned third parties about a danger posed by their patients, with a median number of one warning per professional career. Their warnings affected therapy according to 50 percent of South Carolina/West Virginia therapists. One-third of therapists (35 percent) reported premature patient terminations in therapy because of these warnings.

Nearly all psychiatrists discussed their patients with colleagues, and about 80 percent took the initiative in raising the issue of confidentiality with their patients. Most psychiatrists (77 percent) were willing to provide patients an assurance of confidentiality, but only one-fourth were willing to give an absolute guarantee of confidentiality to their patients.

One-third of psychiatrists (37 percent) thought that patient disclosures were hampered by the legal status of confidentiality. Most (85 percent) South Carolina/West Virginia psychiatrists knew or guessed correctly that there was no privilege in their state.

c. Patient Study

The return rate for the patient sample was 43 percent. The age ranges, median age, and sex distribution of the patients were similar to the Texas group. In South Carolina/West Virginia, the two largest groups were housewives (22 percent) and students (24 percent). While the range of therapy duration and median frequency of sessions were similar to Texas, the median length of therapy was only 8 months.

Forty-one percent of patients thought there was a law prohibiting courtroom disclosure. Confidentiality was an important consideration for half of the patients when starting therapy. More Texas patients than those in South Carolina/West Virginia actually asked about confidentiality (28 percent versus 17 percent), but nearly the same number took steps to ensure confidentiality. Eleven percent would have sought treatment earlier had they known of a privilege statute, but the primary guarantee of privacy was the psychiatrist's ethics and patient's expectation that the psychiatrist-patient relationship was confidential. Thirty-seven percent of the South Carolina/West Virginia group had wondered if there was a privilege law, but only 10 percent had asked their psychiatrist.

Forty-seven percent of the patients had withheld information from their psychiatrist. The most sensitive topics for both groups were sexual thoughts and acts, which accounted for 48 percent of the subjects withheld. There was no reported withholding disclosure of violent acts; about 10 percent had not revealed thoughts of violence.

d. Judicial Study

Of the 74 trial court judges presiding in courts of general jurisdiction (circuit, family, and probate courts) who responded to the questionnaire, 33 (45 percent) reported hearing cases involving admission in court of statements made in confidence to a psychiatrist. Judges hearing domestic relations cases encountered such testimony more frequently than others.

When the question of admitting this evidence arose, most judges (61 percent) thought it important to the case, and most (58 percent) thought it necessary for accurate resolution of contested factual issues. Half thought the information was not available from non-privileged sources; less than a third of the judges thought the question was often raised to encourage settlement; and, only 12 percent thought that the issue was raised often to harrass. Three-quarters of the judges always admitted the confidential communication if relevant. A few (9 percent) imposed a higher standard of relevance, and a quarter would admit it only if unavailable from a nonconfidential source.

3. U. S. Findings

a. Texas versus West Virginia Lay Persons

The lay groups studied in the United States did not differ significantly in age, sex, or marital status. They did differ in occupation (X^2 = 44.40, 4 df, $p < .001$) with greater numbers of professionals and fewer students in the Texas sample, and in willingness to seek treatment for a severe emotional problem (X^2 = 6.70, 1 df, $p < .01$), with Texans being more willing to seek help. Masturbation was the most sensitive topic for both groups before mention was made of privilege or no-privilege conditions. The average nondisclosure rate for both groups doubled under the no-privilege condition. Texans were most sensitive to speeding and work failure under this condition, West Virginians to theft and cheating on income tax. Almost one-quarter of both groups had thought in terms of possible courtroom disclosure of information reported to a therapist. Most Texans thought they were not protected in a murder or custody trial; less than half of the West Virginians thought that a therapist could be forced to testify under the three circumstances suggested in the questionnaire. The responses of both groups to the question of whether privilege existed in their state were not significantly different (X^2 = 1.34, 2 df, n.s.). Their similar responses (most respondents indicated that they did not know) resulted in a larger percentage of Texans (31 percent versus 7 percent) answering correctly. Thus, there is reason to doubt that Texans were significantly more aware of their state's statute.

b. Texas versus South Carolina/West Virginia Patients

It is not known what criteria were employed by therapists in asking patients to complete our questionnaires, but the Texas and South Carolina/West Virginia patients differed in several ways. The Texas group was slightly older (36 versus 33 years), contained more married and less single people, and included a larger number of professional persons, in contrast to the predominance of housewives and students in the South Carolina/West Virginia group. The therapy of the Texas group was more insight-oriented and of considerably longer duration than the South Carolina/West Virginia patients (36 months versus 8 months).

Despite those differences, most of the responses by both groups of patients were similar. Both groups had equal concern about confidentiality when starting treatment, both indicated that the therapist's ethics and the traditional confidentiality of the therapist-patient relationship were of far greater importance as guarantees of confidentiality than a law forbidding disclosure. Few patients in both groups had asked the therapist about confidentiality, and still fewer had asked that steps be taken to ensure confidentiality. Although between a third and a half of the patients wondered if there were a privilege statute, only 10 percent of the patients in both groups actually asked their therapist about the existence of a privilege. Both groups withheld the same type of information, and approximately 10 percent of both groups reported they would have sought treatment earlier had they known of a privilege statute.

To ascertain the effect of patients' belief that they were protected by a privilege statute, patient responses from the two samples were pooled ($n = 120$) and divided into disclosers ($n = 68$) and nondisclosers ($n = 52$) based on whether they had withheld any information at all from their therapists. An equal number (approximately 35 percent) of disclosers and nondisclosers believed that they were protected by a privilege statute.

The most important difference between the two groups' responses was that more of the South Carolina/West Virginia patients (41 percent versus 27 percent) thought, incorrectly, that they had statutory protection against courtroom disclosure by their therapists ($X^2 = 18.98$, 1 df, $p < .001$). Belief in statutory protection did not, however, increase patient disclosure to therapists. ($X^2 = 3.82$, 1 df, n.s.).

c. Texas versus South Carolina/West Virginia Psychiatrists

Although the South Carolina/West Virginia psychiatrists were the same age and had practiced the same length of time as their Texas counterparts, there were important differences in the two groups and the conclusions which may be drawn from their responses. The South Carolina/West Virginia sample is less likely to be representative because of the smaller return rate. The Texas sample was drawn from a large urban population, while nearly half the South Carolina/West Virginia sample practiced in counties of 100,000 or less population.

As would be anticipated from the higher frequency of inpatient and small town practice in the South Carolina/West Virginia group, psychoanalysis and psychoanalytic psychotherapy were less frequently used and supportive therapy and other modalities requiring less personal disclosure were more frequently employed.

Significantly fewer Texas psychiatrists were requested ($X^2 = 9.78$, 1 df, $p < .01$) or required ($X^2 = 57.50$, 1 df, $p < .001$) to testify about their patients in court than their South Carolina/West Virginia counterparts, but that difference may be attributable to South Carolina/West Virginia psychiatrists' involvement in hospital practice and involuntary hospitalization. South Carolina/West Virginia psychiatrists reported more frequent premature terminations after courtroom disclosure than did the Texas group, but the Texas group reported that fewer of their patients who had terminated therapy at the time of the disclosure returned to treatment. In both groups, the number of psychiatrists reporting patient dropouts following psychiatrists' courtroom disclosures was small (9 percent in Texas and 15 percent in South Carolina/West Virginia). Most of the Texas psychiatrists who disclosed did not know if their patients had been damaged, but 25 percent of the South Carolina/West Virginia psychiatrists reported that patients had been harmed.

Both groups of psychiatrists warned third parties endangered by their patients. Both groups reported that warning others frequently affected the patient's therapy. But fewer Texas psychiatrists lost their patients as a result of their warnings.

Psychiatrists reported discussing their patients with other professionals with equal frequency in both surveys. Texas psychiatrists initiated discussion of confidentiality as frequently as the psychiatrists in South Carolina/West Virginia. We had expected more discussion of confidentiality in the states without privilege. As expected, the Texas psychiatrists were more willing to give some assurance of confidentiality, but more of the South Carolina/West Virginia psychiatrists were willing to guarantee absolute confidentiality despite the absence of statutory protection. This may be explained, at least in part, by the responses of psychiatrists who worked at a drug rehabilitation center governed by federal limitations on disclosure.[17]

The fact that less than half of the Texas psychiatrists were aware of their privilege status, while most of the South Carolina/West Virginia psychiatrists were aware they lacked a privilege, may account for the relatively small differences in the reported impact of the privilege laws for those groups. Moreover, many of the Texas psychiatrists and their patients may have been aware that all privilege statutes have exceptions.

d. Texas versus South Carolina/West Virginia Judges

The response rate to the Texas judicial questionnaire (86 percent) was higher than the South Carolina/West Virginia typical response (40 percent) because the Texas judges were contacted personally. South Carolina/West Virginia judges had greater length of experience on the bench (6 yrs. versus 3.5 yrs). There was not a significant difference in the number of Texas judges and South Carolina West Virginian judges who reported hearing cases involving admission of statements made in confidence to a therapist (31 percent versus 45 percent), $X^2 = 2.76$, 1 df, n.s. Most of both groups thought that when a question of admitting such evidence arose, it was important to the case and necessary for accurate resolution of contested factual issues. More of the South Carolina/West Virginia judges thought the information was available from nonprivileged sources and that encouragement to settle and harrassment were significant issues. Most judges in both jurisdictions always admitted such communications if deemed relevant, despite the Texas privilege statute), and few imposed a higher standard of relevance. A substantial number of the South Carolina/West Virginia judges admitted such evidence only if unavailable from nonconfidential sources; only one Texas judge did so.

B. Canadian Study

This phase of empirical research on privilege was designed to gain insight into the effects of a formal privilege in a civil law jurisdiction, Quebec; denominated a professional secret, and lack of a formal privilege in a common law jurisdiction, Ontario. All Quebec questionnaires were in both French and English.

1. Quebec (Civil Law)

The sample for the lay study was a university class in which 97 questionnaires were distributed and 92 were returned (a 95 percent response rate). This was the only group in which one of the authors was present in class at the time a questionnaire was distributed. While the author's presence clearly influenced the return rate, it is not thought that it influenced the responses. Therapist questionnaires were mailed to 427 unselected members of the Canadian Psychiatric Association practicing in Montreal and were returned by 107 (a 25 percent return rate). There were 200 patient questionnaires distributed to the 40 psychiatrists who indicated willingness to distribute them. Of the questionnaires distributed, 70 (35 percent) were returned. Questionnaires were distributed to the 129 Montreal-based judges of the Superior and Provincial Courts in Quebec. Of those, 38 (29 percent) were returned.

a. Lay Study

The respondents ranged in age from 19 to 64, with a median of 24 and an average of 28 years. Seventy-four percent were female, 26 percent male. Nineteen percent were married, nine percent were divorced, and 72 percent had never been married. Eighty percent of the respondents stated that they would consider seeking help from a psychiatrist or psychologist for a serious emotional problem, yet only 36 percent were aware of the existence of the applicable privilege/professional secret.

When asked, without mention of privilege, about topics they would be willing to discuss if relevant in therapy, sexual acts and thoughts, speeding, and theft were the topics in which disclosure was most limited. When asked to respond to those same questions with the assumption that a privilege existed, the response rate varied slightly up and down from category to category, with the biggest change being downward in physical violence and work failure. When asked to respond to these same questions assuming that no privilege applied, the response rate to all questions dropped significantly. Most affected were speeding, sexual acts and thoughts, and work failure.

b. Patient Study

Quebec patients had experienced a median number of 2 years in therapy ranging in duration from a few visits to 20 years. In this group, 59 percent thought there was no privilege or did not know of its existence. Confidentiality had been a consideration for more than half (62 percent) when deciding about therapy, a third (32 percent) asked, and 14 percent took precautions to ensure confidentiality. Again, there was relatively little reliance on legal protection of confidentiality. Only 7 percent of patients indicated that they would have sought treatment earlier had they known of a privilege statute and only 10 percent indicated that they would have been more open.

Nearly half of the patients responding (47.5 percent) indicated they had withheld information from their psychiatrist. Most often withheld were sexual thoughts (28 percent of items withheld) followed by sexual acts (17 percent) and financial issues (17 percent). Eleven percent of the items withheld included violent thoughts toward self or others; only 4 percent of the items were violent acts.

There were significant difference between the lay group and the patient group in age ($X^2 = 2.70$, 151 df, $p < .01$), marital status ($X^2 = 22.50$, 2 df, $p < .001$) and occupation ($X^2 = 29.20$, 3 df, $p < .001$), but no significant differences in sex distribution ($X^2 = .03$, 1 df, n.s.). The age range was similar, but there was a 13 year disparity between the median age of the patient group (37 years) and the lay group (24 years). There was not a significant difference in the number of patients and lay persons who thought there was a privilege ($X^2 = .15$, 1 df, n.s.).

Lay persons were most unwilling to discuss theft, masturbation, and other sexual acts when privilege was not mentioned. Speeding, masturbation, work failure, and other sexual acts became the most sensitive issues under the no-privilege condition.

c. Therapist Study

The respondents had practiced a median of 16 years. Less than half had full-time private practices, and one-fifth had exclusively outpatient practices. They utilized a variety of types of therapy. Twenty-seven percent employed psychoanalysis, 86 percent used psychoanalytic psychotherapy, 78 percent used supportive therapy, and 24 percent used behavior therapy.

The average number of patients seen per week was 26 and the median frequency of visits per patient per week was one.

Thirty-five percent of the respondents had been requested to disclose confidential information in court. Twenty-one percent of these requested (7 percent of the entire group) were ultimately compelled to reveal the information. Nine therapists indicated that the disclosures did cause psychological harm to patients, but only one therapist opined that the therapeutic process was impaired. Seven therapists reported premature termination of therapy because of the disclosure.

Only 54 percent of the respondents were aware of the existence of an applicable privilege/professional secret in Quebec. Twenty-two percent stated that the current status of the law limits patient disclosures in therapy.

Sixty-eight percent took the initiative, from time to time, to raise the issue of confidentiality with patients. When asked by patients about confidentiality, these therapists responded in a variety of ways ranging from "I will not disclose without your written consent" to "I will not disclose unless ordered to do so by a court."

d. Judicial Study

Nineteen judges, 54 percent of those responding, reported hearing a case involving the admission of a confidential communication to a psychotherapist. The dockets of these judges nearly always included some domestic cases, thus confirming the results of informal interviews that domestic cases account for the greatest frequency of cases involving attempted disclosure of confidential communications to a psychotherapist. In no instance did a judge report compelling disclosure in the absence of the patient's consent, raising a discrepancy between the responses of therapists who reported being compelled to testify and these judges that we cannot reconcile with certainty. The discrepancy may have several explanations. Judges who forced disclosure may not have been included in our sample. Or, psychiatrists may have responded to the questions about forced disclosure by commenting that disclosure was forced if they objected to disclosure, even if made with the patient's consent.

2. Ontario (Common Law)

The lay sample for Ontario was a university class. Of 100 questionnaires distributed, 58 were returned. The therapist questionnaires were mailed to 445 unselected members of the Canadian Psychiatric Association practicing in Ontario and returned by 81 (an 18 percent return rate). Psychiatrists who indicated willingness to do so were sent questionnaires and asked to distribute them to five patients each. There were 58 responses to the 100 questionnaires presumably distributed. questionnaires were distributed to the 97 Toronto-based judges of the High Court of Justice for Ontario, the Ontario provincial Courts (Civil and Family Divisions), and the County and District Courts of Ontario. There were 32 questionnaires returned (a return rate of 33 percent).

a. Lay Study

The lay respondents ranged in age from 18 to 60, with a median of 23 years. Seventy-one percent were female. Ten percent were married, 12 percent were divorced, and 78 percent had never been married.

Although 93 percent of the respondents indicated that they would seek help from a psychiatrist or psychologist for a serious emotional problem, only eight percent were aware or guessed correctly that no privilege existed.

This group was asked, without any mention of a privilege, if, having sought help, and if relevant in therapy, they would discuss subjects such as sexual fantasies, physical violence, masturbation, work failure, and theft. Sexual acts and thoughts were the topics on which disclosure was most limited. They were then asked to respond to the same questions with the assumption that a privilege existed. A slight change in the responses occurred, in the direction of less disclosure, perhaps indicating the absence of any prior consideration of the need for privilege. When asked to respond to the same questions under a no privilege condition, the response rates to all questions dropped significantly ($X^2 = 11.88$, 1 df, $p < .001$). The items most affected were speeding, physical violence, and work failure.

b. Patient Study

Most Ontario patients had considerable experience in therapy. The median duration of therapy was 2 years, with a range from less than one month to 20 years. Of the group, 61 percent thought there was no privilege or did not know. Confidentiality had been a consideration for nearly half (46 percent) when deciding about treatment, but only half that number (24 percent) had inquired and 16 percent of the entire group took steps to determine the limits of confidentiality. Patients indicated a much heavier reliance on their therapist's ethics than on a statutory guarantee. None of the respondents indicated that they would have sought treatment earlier had they known of a privilege statute; six percent indicated that they would have been more open.

One-third of respondents had withheld information from their psychiatrists. Most commonly withheld were sexual thoughts (34 percent of items withheld) with thoughts of violence and sexual acts each accounting for 17 percent of items withheld. In this group, 6 percent of the items withheld involved violent acts; possible crimes and drug use comprised 10 percent taken together.

A significant difference was found between the lay group and the patient group in age ($X^2 = 21.7$, 110 df, $p < .001$) marital status ($X^2 = 22$, 2 df, $p < .001$), and occupation ($X^2 = 55$, 3 df, $p < .001$), but no significant difference was found in sex distribution ($X^2 = .04$, 1 df, n.s.). The age range was comparable, but the median age of the patient group was 36 years, versus 23 years for the lay group. There was not a significant difference in the number of patients and lay persons who thought there was a privilege ($X^2 = .037$, 1 df, n.s.).

Lay persons were most unwilling to discuss masturbation, sexual fantasies, and cheating on income tax when privilege was not mentioned, but became essentially equally nondisclosing on all subjects under the no-privilege condition (speeding became the most sensitive issue).

c. Therapist Study

The therapists responding had a median length of practice of 13 years. Less than half (42 percent) had full-time private practices, and only 25 percent had exclusively outpatient practices. Psychoanalytic psychotherapy was the most commonly used modality (63 percent), while 60 percent employed supportive psychotherapy. The median number of patients seen per week was 25, and the median frequency of outpatient visits per week was one.

Forty-two percent of the respondents had been requested to disclose confidential information in court and 28 percent of those asked (12 percent of the entire group) were ultimately required to reveal this information. Nearly half (43 percent) of the therapists who disclosed were of the opinion that judicial disclosure caused psychological harm to their patients. Twenty-two percent of the patients terminated therapy prematurely because of the disclosure.

Slightly more than half (54 percent) of the respondents believed or guessed correctly that there was no privilege limiting compelled judicial disclosure of confidential communications between therapist and patient. The same percent indicated that the current law limits patient disclosures in therapy.

Eighty-one percent of the respondents took the initiative, at times, to raise the issues of confidentiality with patients. In response to questions by patients about confidentiality, the therapists had a broad range of responses ranging from "all this can be subpoenaed," "I'll not tell unless others are endangered," to "I'll never tell."

d. Judicial Study

Nine of the judges (28 percent) reported hearing a case involving the admission of a confidential communication to a psychotherapist. Because 84 percent of the judges who responded heard some domestic cases and 96 percent heard some criminal cases, it was difficult to ascertain from their dockets which of these categories accounted for the greater experience. The response to our question about significant cases raising this issue resulted in the mentioning of child custody (2), criminal (1), general domestic (1), and personal injury (1), again providing little basis for generalization about the category of cases. The other bases for distinguishing categories of cases, a review of reported cases, and informal discussions with judges, point in the direction of child custody/domestic cases as accounting for the greatest number of cases in which this issue arises.

The judges indicated that in no case in which the admission of a statement made in confidence by a patient to his psychotherapist arose was the statement admitted without the patient's consent. Thus, even in the absence of a formal privilege, psychotherapist-patient confidences seem to be respected in the courts with a *de facto* privilege. As in the civil law study, the responses of the judges differ from psychiatrists' reports that they were forced to testify. Again, the population of respondents may not overlap or their definitions of patient consent may vary.

3. Canadian Findings

a. Quebec versus Ontario Lay Persons

There were significant differences between the Canadian lay groups. The return rate for Quebec was considerably higher probably because the questionnaires were distributed to students directly by one of the investigators ($X^2 = 35.42$, 1 df, $p < .001$). Age range and mean age were similar, as was sex distribution. The two groups did differ significantly in terms of occupation, and a significantly larger number of Ontarians (93 percent versus 80 percent) indicated willingness to seek help for a severe emotional problem (X^2 = 4.60, 1 df, p < .02). Masturbation and other sexual acts were the most sensitive topics for both groups when no mention was made of any condition. Speeding became the most sensitive topic when a no-privilege condition was suggested. One-quarter or less of the respondents had thought in terms of possible courtroom disclosure of information imparted to a psychologist or psychiatrist. Both groups assumed that less protection of confidentiality existed if a capital offense was involved than if there was a custody fight.

Canadian lay persons were significantly less aware of the status of privilege than Canadian patients (24 percent of lay persons versus 40 percent of patients) (X^2 = 7.20, 1 df, p < .01).

As in the American sample, there were considerable differences between the lay group and the patient group. The lay group was significantly younger (t = 4.21, 263 df, p < .001) and consisted of more single persons (X^2 = 22, 2 df, p < .001), had fewer professionals and many more students (X^2 = 55, 3 df, p < .001). There was not a significant difference in the male:female ratio.

b. Quebec versus Ontario Patients

Return rates for patient questionnaires were similar, as were patients' median age, median duration of therapy, and median frequency of therapy. There was no significant difference in sex distribution, marital status, or occupation. Forty percent of both groups thought there was a law protecting patients' communications from disclosure to psychiatrists in court. Quebec patients were more concerned with confidentiality, but not significantly so. Roughly the same percentage of patients in each group asked about confidentiality and took steps to ensure it. Few Quebec patients and no Ontario patients would have sought treatment sooner had they known of a privilege. Both groups valued professional ethics above a statutory guarantee of confidentiality. Fewer Ontario patients wondered if there was a privilege statute. Quebec patients withheld information from their therapists more than Ontarians, but not significantly so. Sexual thoughts were the most sensitive topics for both. The existence of a privilege statute would have encouraged a few more Quebec patients to be more open than Ontario patients (10 percent versus 6 percent).

c. Quebec versus Ontario Therapists

Because the return rate for both groups of therapists was low, the sample may not be representative of each population. However, the similarity of these data to the data from the American studies suggests that they may well reflect the general characteristics of psychiatrists practicing in North America.

There was no significant difference in questionnaire return rate, age, sex, type of practice, type of psychotherapy, average number of patients seen per week, or frequency of outpatient visits.

There was no significant difference in the frequency with which therapists were asked to make courtroom disclosure, however, requests were rare. The median therapist in each group had never been requested to disclose in court. A few therapists from each group were forced to disclose (6 percent in Quebec, 12 percent in Ontario), but there was no significant difference ($X^2 = 1.80$, 1 df, n.s.) between the two groups. Of the therapists who did disclose, from 30 to 43 percent reported that patients were harmed psychologically and from 22 to 23 percent of patients who were in therapy at the time of the disclosure terminated treatment prematurely.

Quebec therapists warned endangered third parties significantly less often than did Ontario therapists (20 versus 37 percent) ($X^2 = 4.27$, 1 df, $< .05$), but their warnings were infrequent, averaging one warning in 6 years for Quebec therapists and one per 2.6 years for Ontario therapists. Significantly fewer Quebec therapists than Ontario therapists discussed patients with colleagues (84 percent versus 96 percent) ($X^2 = 6.10$, 1 df, $p < .02$) and significantly fewer took the initiative in discussing confidentiality. However, a significantly greater number of Quebec therapists were willing to guarantee absolute confidence (51 percent versus 20 percent) ($X^2 = 14.76$, 2 df, $p < .001$).

A greater number of Ontario therapists thought that patient communication was limited by the status of confidentiality in their province, but this was of marginal significance ($X^2 = 3.8$, 1 df, $p < .06$. That this difference was not based on ignorance of the law is demonstrated by the lack of significant difference between Quebec and Ontario therapists' current knowledge of the status of privilege in the province (54 percent versus 57 percent) ($X^2 = 3.18$, 1 df, n.s.).

d. Quebec versus Ontario Judges

Response rates to the questionnaires were similar. There was a large apparent difference in Quebec and Ontario judges' experience with the question of admitting confidential psychotherapist-patient communications (50 percent versus 28 percent), but because of the small number of respondents, the difference was not statistically significant ($X^2 = 2.60$, 1 df, n.s.). Although Quebec judges less often thought such communications relevant and more often thought that the same information was available from nonprivileged sources, these differences were also not statistically significant. The most important finding was that despite differences in the law, judges in both jurisdictions dealt with confidential communications between psychiatrist and patient in much the same way. Of the nine Ontario judges who had dealt with confidential communication issues, five (56 percent) admitted this evidence only with the patient's consent despite the nonexistence of privilege, which is not significantly different from Quebec judges. Of the 20 Quebec judges who had dealt with the issue, eight (40 percent) admitted these communications only with the patient's consent. The most common issues were child custody and malpractice.

C. Pooled Data

Pooling the data from all three studies sheds further light on the hypotheses under investigation.

1. Pooled Lay Studies (See Table 5)

The response rates for the Texas and West Virginia samples are estimates; questionnaires were distributed to several faculty members at colleges in those states and accurate tallies of their distribution were not kept. The estimated return rates are high enough (69 percent) that a fairly representative sample of each population should exist. Because four different geographical areas were sampled, the conclusions are generalizable.

The respondents had approximately equal age ranges and had similar median and mean ages. There was no significant difference between the mean age of any group so the entire group of lay persons were detected by the Student's T test. There were significant differences in sex distribution ($X^2 = 25$, 1 df, $p < .001$), marital status ($X^2 = 15.9$, 6 df, $p < .02$), and occupation (X^2 = 85, 12 df, $p < .001$). Three of the four groups consisted largely of unmarried female students in large urban areas. The modal lay person was a single 23 year-old female student.

There was a positive attitude in all groups toward seeking psychological/psychiatric help, although there were significant differences between groups (X^2 = 11, 2 df, $p < .02$). Most persons in all groups indicated that they had no idea if a privilege existed in their state or province, and most did not consider the possibility that information disclosed might be revealed to a third party.

Three-quarters or more of the persons queried indicated that they would discuss speeding, sexual fantasies, masturbation, other sexual acts, physical violence, work failure, cheating on income tax, and theft with a psychologist or psychiatrist if it was important, but half or less were willing to reveal the same information under the no-privilege condition, a statistically significant difference (X^2 = 15.88, 3 df, $p < .01$). Only 25 percent of lay persons knew or guessed correctly the status of privilege in their state or province. Canadians more often thought they were protected than did Americans, with Ontarians the most confident of this protection despite the absence of a privilege in their province.

2. Pooled Patient Data (See Table 6)

Although the return rate was only 38 percent overall, the number of populations sampled make it likely that a broad, cross-sectional representation of patients in psychotherapy was obtained.

The patients did not differ significantly from lay persons in sex distribution, but did differ significantly from the lay group in age (t = 6.75, 595 df, $p < .001$), marital status (X^2 = 37.42, 2 df, $p < .001$), and occupation (X^2 = 98.80, 3 df, $p < .001$), and were themselves quite heterogeneous from group to group. Although the modal patient was a married woman in her mid-30s, the patients ranged in age from 16 to 65, a 44 year age span. The modal patient had been in therapy once a week for approximately two years. Although 70 percent of the patients were women, relatively few indicated their sole occupation as housewife. The largest single occupational category was professional (26 percent).

About a third of the patients knew or guessed correctly the status of the law in their state or province concerning courtroom disclosures by psychiatrists or psychologists, significantly more than the lay sample (X^2 = 19.26, 1 df, $p < .001$). Although most patients (53 percent) were concerned about confidentiality, only a quarter indicated that it was a great concern. The implication was that confidentiality but not privilege was accepted as a given right. Thus, only a quarter of patients asked their psychiatrists about confidentiality and only 15 percent took an active step toward assuring confidentiality. Only one patient out of every seventeen would have sought treatment earlier had he or she known of a privilege statute, and less than a fifth (19 percent) would have relied on this statute as a principal guarantor of confidentiality.

Between a third and nearly half of all patients (41 percent) had withheld information from their therapist. Sexual thoughts and acts were the categories of information most frequently withheld. Five persons (2 percent of patients) reported withholding discussion of violent acts. Nine percent withheld thoughts of violence toward self or others. Only a small percentage (13 percent) indicated that a privilege law would have enabled them to be more open in therapy. Despite patients' general knowledge of privilege in their state or province, there was no relationship between the number of patients withholding information and the existence of privilege in their state of province ($X^2 = 0.68$, 1 df, n.s.). Thus, from the patients' viewpoint, the utilitarian argument for privilege is not strong. Patients clearly expect their therapists not to discuss them outside the office, but that expectation is based on professional discretion and not on a legal limitation or guarantee.

It has been argued that lack of privilege keeps out of treatment those persons who are the greatest danger to themselves or others, but that argument hardly seems justifiable in view of the fact that so few patients avoided discussion of violent acts.

It is possible that the patient data was biased because it involved patient selection by therapists in addition to self-selection by patients. Thus, therapists may have excluded patients with histories of violence against self or others, not wanting to traumatize or unduly arouse these persons. To examine for the possibility of therapist bias, data derived from a fortunate accident was included. Patient questionnaires were accidentally distributed to a West Virginia lay group (the lay questionnaires were distributed to a different group of students at a later time). Of the 100 patient questionnaires accidentally distributed to lay persons, 53 were returned. Of those 53, 12 had been completed by persons who were or had been in therapy (see Table 6A). This group differs from other patient groups in its relatively short reported duration of therapy (median = 3 months), suggesting that therapists tended to select patients with whom they had stable long-term relationships.

In this group of 12 persons, 67 percent were concerned about the confidentiality of their treatment, as compared with 53 percent of the patients in the therapist-selected group (X^2 = 1.66, 1 df, n.s.); not a significant difference. Fifty percent asked the psychiatrist about confidentiality, which was not significantly different (X^2 = 1.90, 1 df, n.s.) from the others' 27 percent rate of asking the psychiatrist. Three of the 12 respondents took steps to ensure confidentiality, which was not significantly different from the 15 percent rate reported by the therapist selected patients. A significantly greater percentage of the accidentally discovered patients would have sought treatment earlier had they known of a privilege statute (X^2 = 4.67, 1 df, $p < .05$). There was no significant difference in the percentage of each group that asked if there was a privilege, in the percentage who withheld information, or in the percentage of persons who would have been more open had they known of a privilege statute (X^2 = 2.80, 1 df, n.s.).

Thus, it may reasonably be concluded that psychiatrists' selection of patients did not result in strongly biased responses. The only item that achieved significance was the issue of seeking treatment earlier. Perhaps being closer to the beginning of their treatment, these people were more aware of their own hesitancy, while those who had been in treatment for greater lengths of time may in retrospect have seen themselves as less hesitant. If one-third is accepted as a more accurate percentage of persons who would have sought treatment earlier, a privilege statute might be a more positive influence on prompt treatment-seeking than the rest of the data would suggest, but the small size of this sample makes it difficult to generalize.

3. Pooled Therapist Data (See Table 4)

Of the 1306 questionnaires distributed, 320 (25 percent) were returned. At that return rate, a representative sampling of psychiatric practices in North America has been accomplished, especially in view of having sampled five different geographical areas. The psychiatrists sampled, although in different practice settings, were largely (82 percent) in full-time practice. The modal therapist was a 45 year old man, in practice for 13 years, seeing 32 patients a week in psychotherapy. Patients were seen once a week in psychoanalytic psychotherapy or supportive psychotherapy.

Only 16 percent of the respondents used psychoanalysis as a means of treatment, and few psychoanalysts employed psychoanalysis exclusively.

Therapists in Quebec, with its professional secret, were asked to disclose in court significantly less often ($X^2 = 21.30$, 1 df, $p < .001$) and least often forced to disclose ($X^2 = 3.5$, 1 df, n.s.). The South Carolina/West Virginia group, which lacked privilege and involved more hospital practice, was significantly more often asked to disclose ($X^2 = 4.20$, 1 df, $p < .05$), and significantly more often forced to disclose ($X^2 = 39.9$, 1 df, $p < .001$). Texas, with its new privilege statute, and Ontario, without privilege, were essentially similar, occupying a position intermediate between Quebec and South Carolina/West Virginia.

Significantly fewer Canadian psychiatrists warned endangered third parties than did their American counterparts ($X^2 = 11.54$, 1 df, $p < .001$) and significantly fewer Quebec psychiatrists warned than did Ontario psychiatrists ($X^2 = 4.7$, 1 df, $p < .05$). Fewer Canadian psychiatrists reported discussing patients with colleagues than did American psychiatrists, but the difference was not significant. Significantly fewer Quebec psychiatrists discussed patients with colleagues than Ontario psychiatrists ($X^2 = 6.10$, 1 df, $p < .02$). U.S. and Ontario psychiatrists did not differ on the frequency with which they took the initiative in discussing confidentiality with patients (81 versus 91 percent), but Quebec psychiatrists took the initiative significantly less often ($X^2 = 5.52$, 1 df, $p < .02$). Although Quebec psychiatrists were protected by the professional secret, there was only a marginally significant difference between Quebec and Ontario psychiatrists ($X^2 = 3.80$, 1 df, $p < .06$) when asked if they thought that the present status of confidentiality limited what patients told them. Only 54 percent of the Quebec group and 67 percent of the Ontario group actually knew or guessed correctly the status of the law in their province.

Nearly half (45 percent) of the psychiatrists had been asked to disclose in court, but only 39 (14 percent) were forced to disclose by the court. Others seemed to have disclosed over patients' objections, presumably in relation to involuntary hospitalization. A request to disclose confidential communications in court occurred approximately once for each 13 years of practice. Eighteen therapists knew of patients who had been harmed by courtroom disclosures, but most therapists testified about patients who were no longer in therapy with them, so that the harm done to patients may be under-reported. Therapy was frequently affected by courtroom disclosures (sometimes negatively and sometimes positively) and premature terminations also seemed to be frequent. That courtroom disclosures do not always ruin therapeutic relationships is attested by the return of 47 percent of patients to therapy with the same therapist.

Nearly all therapists (91 percent) discussed their patients with colleagues, and four of five took the initiative in discussing confidentiality. Twenty-eight percent of therapists were willing to guarantee absolute confidentiality; many of those in a state or province without privilege. About a quarter (28 percent) of therapists in all jurisdictions thought that patients were constrained from complete openness by the limitation of the status of confidentiality. Quebec psychiatrists most often guaranteed confidentiality (51 percent) and thought least compromised by the status of privilege in their province. Therapists in states/provinces without privilege reported significantly more often (X^2 = 16.38, 1 df, $p < .001$) that their patients' openness was hampered. Overall, only 60 percent of therapists knew or guessed correctly the status of privilege in their state or province, ranging from a low of 45 percent in Texas, where the law had recently changed, to a high of 85 percent in South Carolina/West Virginia, where judicially compelled disclosure was most frequent.

4. Pooled Judicial Data (See Table 5)

The judicial studies were conducted in different ways. The questionnaire for Texas judges was administered through individual interviews by law students. Judges in South Carolina/West Virginia, Ontario, and Quebec responded to questionnaires that were mailed to them. Nearly 80 percent of the judges who responded in all studies were from urban jurisdictions. An attempt was made to categorize judges according to the predominant type of case with which they dealt, but this was unsuccessful outside of Texas. While Texas judges' jurisdiction was divided between domestic relations, criminal, probate/mental health, and miscellaneous civil, the distinctions were not always as clear in other jurisdictions.

Judges' response rate to the questionnaires ranged from 86 percent in Texas to 29 percent in Quebec. The Texas response rate was significantly higher than the other response rates (X^2 = 60, 3 df, $p < .001$). Response rates in the other three jurisdictions were not significantly different (X^2 = 4.26, 2 df, n.s.).

Overall, 40 percent of judges had dealt with the question of admitting information from psychotherapeutic interactions. There was no statistical difference in the number of judges, in the four areas, who encountered the issue (X^2 = 6.55, 3 df, n.s.). The range was 28 percent (Ontario) to 54 percent (Quebec). It was not possible to tabulate the number of times per judge the issue of admitting this material arose. Estimates by judges ranged from none to 25 cases. It was also not possible to analyze statistically the data concerning the relationship between the type of case heard and the frequency with which the issue of admitting material from therapy arose. From the interviews and a review of reported cases, however, it appears that the issue arose most commonly in domestic relations cases involving child custody.

Most of the judges queried (60 percent) thought that when a question of admitting confidential communication arose, the information involved was important to the case; 48 percent thought it necessary for accurate resolution of contested factual issues, but the same percentage of judges also thought the information was available from nonprivileged sources. Few judges thought that the question was raised to encourage settlement (21 percent) or to harrass (10 percent).

When a confidential communication between a psychotherapist and a patient was sought to be admitted in evidence, 62 percent of the judges always admitted it if relevant; 13 percent imposed a higher standard of relevance, and 25 percent admitted it only if unavailable from a nonconfidential source. One Texas judge and three Quebec judges never admitted such information. Overall, there was no statistical difference between judges' means of dealing with the issue despite the differing laws concerning confidential communication in the jurisdictions studied (X^2 = 7.38, 6 df, n.s.). A significant statistical difference between U.S. and Canadian judges was found on only one issue. U.S. judges thought that seeking to introduce confidential communications in evidence was more likely to be associated with attempts at forcing a settlement than did Canadian judges (X^2 = 9.10, 2 df, $p < .02$). This likely corresponds to a difference in the operation of the adversarial system in these countries. Even so, only a fifth of U.S. judges thought this was a frequent occurrence.

III. CONCLUSION

A review of empirical studies leads to the following conclusions:

1. Lay persons and patients in psychotherapy express concern about the confidentiality of patient-therapist communications. The lay persons surveyed indicate that they would be significantly less disclosing to a therapist if there were no privilege (X^2 = 10.3, 1 df, $p < .01$). This was

not so great a concern that many lay persons were aware of the status of privilege in their state or province. Most lay persons (64 percent) said they did not know, and only 20 percent actually knew, or guessed correctly, the status of privilege.

Patients indicated clearly that what was most important as a guarantee of confidentiality was their trust of the psychiatrist as a person and a professional with an ethical duty to maintain confidentiality and not any legal guarantee. Interview studies of psychiatric outpatients and inpatients conducted by Appelbaum[18] and Schmidt[19] shed further light on the confidentiality versus privilege issue. They found that patients in psychiatric treatment were less concerned about disclosure than they were about the circumstances of the disclosure. Disclosure to other helping professionals was quite acceptable. Disclosure that would potentially humiliate or demean them was not. Thus, the norm was not so much one of disclosure versus nondisclosure, but disclosure in the service of the patient versus disclosure that might harm the patient's self-esteem or self-interest.

2. It seems very unlikely that privilege or lack of privilege deters individuals from seeking psychological help or psychiatric treatment. The best evidence for this conclusion is that there was no increase in psychotherapeutic visits to psychiatrists following passage of the Texas privilege statute. This conclusion is further supported by the observation that both the lay public and patients in therapy alike are relatively unaware of the status of privilege. If privilege was a very important consideration, it is likely that potential patients would take the trouble to become informed about privilege, but for the most part, they do not.

3. The study substantiates that a small number of persons (6 percent) would have sought therapy earlier had they known of a privilege statute. It could be argued that the sample did not include persons for whom privilege is the most important, such as sex offenders or persons prone to violence, most of whom may not be treated by the ordinary psychiatric practitioner. It was thought unwise to ask the patients studied if violent thoughts or acts or criminal acts constituted an important problem for fear that the return rate would be compromised. Instead, a more general question was asked as to whether these issues had been withheld, hoping to address the same information. Moreover, communications concerning treatment involving violence and abuse of children comes within an exception to the privilege in most jurisdictions.

4. The argument that lack of privilege impairs the quality of treatment

because it reinforces conscious and unconscious resistances is based on the psychoanalytic model of therapy—that patients need to drop all censorship to profit from treatment. However, psychoanalysis is a relatively rare form of treatment and persons who are ordinarily candidates for psychoanalysis are not likely to be in certain categories of litigation such as civil commitment or criminal proceedings. To be a candidate for psychoanalysis ordinarily requires a relatively stable life situation and candidates for psychoanalysis ordinarily have emotional disturbances that do not involve great likelihood of violence toward self or others. Although, patients in psychoanalysis might be involved in divorce litigation concerning child custody, most of the therapies employed by the psychiatrists surveyed do not require full disclosure. Primarily, they involve discussion of the presenting problems and their consequences. The authors' studies suggest, furthermore, that there is little relationship between patients withholding information from their therapist and the status of privilege. Forty-one percent of patients withheld information from their therapist, and seemed to do so for reasons unrelated to fear of public disclosure. No relationship was found between the legal status of privilege and patients' disclosure in therapy ($X^2 = 0.68$, 1 df, n.s.).

5. There is evidence that therapists' courtroom testimony both compromises therapy and causes premature termination of therapy. It is not know if those who terminated therapy prematurely were dangerous to themselves or others. Some of the therapists testifying undoubtedly revealed in court confidential communications in an effort to secure involuntary hospitalization by testifying about patients' dangerousness. That breach of trust probably permanently alienated some of the patients. However, a number of therapists indicated that patients were reassured by their disclosure or threat of disclosure of potential harm to self or others.

6. Some of the therapists who made courtroom disclosures reported that patients were often harmed psychologically by their disclosure. The frequency of this harm occurring may have been under-reported, however, because most of the persons about whom therapists testified were no longer in treatment. These disclosures, however, were relatively infrequent. It may be inferred that the most common damage was loss of self-esteem due to loss of child custody.

7. The judicial studies do not suggest that judges find privilege a great impediment to truth-finding at trial, or for that matter, that information from therapeutic encounters is uniformly important at trial. Although

judges see most attempts to introduce confidential communication as legitimate, they find that the same information is often obtainable from other sources.

In summary, these empirical studies suggest that while confidentiality is important in therapeutic relationships, privilege is not. Psychotherapists, as competent professionals or as caring friends, are expected to exercise discretion in what they reveal. Patients reacted positively when therapists made disclosures that helped them regain control of themselves or helped to protect others. When information that was experienced as embarrassing or personally damaging was revealed, no matter what the reason, the therapeutic relationship was endangered and the persons who trusted in them were often harmed psychologically.

REFERENCES

1. Singer, *Informed Consent: Consequences for Response Rate and Response Quality in Social Surveys,* 43 Am. Social Review 144 (1978).
2. Rosen, *Why Clients Relinquish Their Rights to Privacy Under Sign-away Pressures,* 8 Prof. Psychologist 17 (1977).
3. Del Rio, *The Ellsberg Psychoanalytic Situation,* 5 Int. J. Psychoanalytic Psychotherapy 349 (1976).
4. Appelbaum, Kapen, Walters, et al, *Confidentiality: An Empirical Test of the Utilitarian Perspective,* 12 *Bull. of the Am. Academy of Psychiatry and Law* 109 (1984).
5. Schmid, Appelbaum, Roth, et al, *Confidentiality in Psychiatry: A Study of the Patient's View,* 34 Hosp. and Comm. Psychiatry 353 (1983).
6. Suarez and Balcanoff, *Massachusetts Psychiatry and Privileged Communication,* 15 Arch. Gen. Psychiatry 619 (1966).
7. Comment, *Functional Overlap Between the Lawyer and Other Professionals: Its Implications for the Privilege Communication Doctrine,* 71 Yale L.J. 1226 (1962).
8. Note, *Where the Public Peril Begins: A Survey of Psychotherapists to Determine the Effects of Tarasoff,* 31 Stanford L. Rev. 165 (1978).
9. Tarasoff v. Regents of the University of California, 17 Cal 3d 425, 529 P2d 334, 131 Cal. Rptr. 14 (1976).
10. Shuman and Weiner, *The Privilege Study: An Empirical Examination of the Psychotherapist-Patient Privilege,* 60 N.C.L.Rev. 893 (1983).
11. Weiner and Shuman, *Privilege—A Comparative Study,* 12 J. Psych & Law 373 (1984).
12. Shuman, Weiner, and Pinard, *The Privilege Study (Part III): Psychotherapist-Patient Communications in Canada,* 9 Int'l. J. Law and Psych. 393 (1987).
13. p values refer to probability. A p value of less than .05 (p .05) is generally accepted as statistically significant. It means that an event can occur by chance less than 5 times in 100; odds of less than one in 20.

14. df means degrees of freedom, indicating at what place a statistical table was entered to estimate probability; n.s. means not statistically significant.
15. Psychoanalytic therapy differs from psychoanalysis in lesser frequency of visits and less reliance on free association. Sessions are usually focused on present problems in living as they are reflected in the therapist-patient relationship.
16. S.D. means standard deviation; a measure of the variation in a sample.
17. 42 U.S.C. § 290ee-3.
18. Appelbaum, *supra* note 4.
19. Schmid, *supra*, note 5.

TABLE 1
STUDENT PRIVILEGE QUESTIONNAIRE

INSTRUCTIONS: Please answer all appropriate questions in the order they are asked. Do not read the next question until you have recorded your answer to the preceding question. Do not change your answer to a question once you have read the following question.

QUESTIONS

1. If you had a serious emotional problem would you consider seeking help from a psychologist or a psychiatrist? ☐ YES ☐ NO If "NO" go on to question 4.
2. If you would consider seeking such help and the following subjects were important, would you reveal them to the psychologist or psychiatrist?
   a. Your driving in excess of the speed limit ☐ YES ☐ NO
   b. Your sexual fantasies ☐ YES ☐ NO
   c. Your physical violence to another person ☐ YES ☐ NO
   d. Your experience with masturbation ☐ YES ☐ NO
   e. Your work failures or inadequacies ☐ YES ☐ NO
   f. Your sexual activities other than masturbation ☐ YES ☐ NO
   g. Your cheating on income tax ☐ YES ☐ NO
   h. Your taking of another's property ☐ YES ☐ NO
3. When you answered questions 1 and 2 did you consider that your psychologist or psychiatrist might be asked about your conversations with him:
   a. By your medical insurance carrier? ☐ YES ☐ NO
   b. By a state agency? ☐ YES ☐ NO
   c. By a potential employer? ☐ YES ☐ NO
   d. By a lawyer in a trial? ☐ YES ☐ NO
4. Is there a law in Texas that prevents a court from forcing a psychologist or psychiatrist called as a witness at a trial to state what his patient told him: ☐ YES ☐ NO ☐ DON'T KNOW
5. If there is such a law, may the psychologist or psychiatrist be required to testify in any of the following situations:
   a. You are charged with murder and what you told the psychologist or psychiatrist proves that you did it. ☐ YES ☐ NO
   b. You sue someone for emotional injuries you suffered in an accident but the psychiatrist or psychologist thinks your problems started before the accident. ☐ YES ☐ NO
   c. You and your spouse seek a divorce and fight over child custody and some things you told the psychologist or psychiatrist will not help your case. ☐ YES ☐ NO
6. Assume that the law in Texas does prevent a court from forcing a psychologist or psychiatrist called as a witness at trial to state what his patient told him and the following subjects were important to your discussions with him or her. Would you reveal to the psychologist or psychiatrist:
   a. Your driving in excess of the speed limit? ☐ YES ☐ NO

b. Your sexual fantasies? ☐ YES ☐ NO
c. Your physical violence to another person? ☐ YES ☐ NO
d. Your experience with masturbation? ☐ YES ☐ NO
e. Your work failures or inadequacies? ☐ YES ☐ NO
f. Your sexual activities other than masturbation? ☐ YES ☐ NO
g. Your cheating on income tax? ☐ YES ☐ NO
h. Your taking of another's property? ☐ YES ☐ NO

7. If there were no such law and a psychiatrist or a psychologist could be forced to tell in court what you revealed in therapy, would it affect your discussion with the psychiatrist or psychologist of:
a. Your driving in excess of the speed limit? ☐ YES ☐ NO
b. Your sexual fantasies? ☐ YES ☐ NO
c. Your physical violence to another person? ☐ YES ☐ NO
d. Your experience with masturbation? ☐ YES ☐ NO
e. Your work failures or inadequacies? ☐ YES ☐ NO
f. Your sexual activities other than masturbation? ☐ YES ☐ NO
g. Your cheating on income tax? ☐ YES ☐ NO
h. Your taking of another's property? ☐ YES ☐ NO

Age: ____ Male ☐ Female ☐ Marital Status: S ☐ M ☐ D ☐ W ☐ Occupation ________

TABLE 2
PATIENT PRIVILEGE QUESTIONNAIRE

Do you think there is a law which prohibits psychiatrists from disclosing what patients tell them to:

a) the psychiatrist's friends . . . . Yes _____ No _____ Don't Know _____

b) the psychiatrist's professional colleagues . . . . Yes _____ No _____ Don't Know _____

c) a court of law . . . . Yes _____ No _____ Don't Know _____

Was the confidentiality of the doctor-patient relationship a consideration for you when you first started thinking about therapy? . . . . Yes _____ No _____

If your answer to (2) was YES, was it (check one)

a) A *very* important consideration (you had great concern about the privacy of your communication) . . . . _________

b) A *not* important consideration (you wondered briefly if your communication to the doctor might be disclosed but didn't think further about it) . . . . _________

c) Somewhere between (a) and (b) . . . . _________

If you were concerned about the confidentiality of the relationship, did you ask the doctor about it? . . . . Yes _____ No _____

Did you take any steps to insure the confidentiality of the relationship, like ask the doctor not to keep written records or obtain his word that he would not disclose what you told him? . . . . Yes _____ No _____

a) What did you do? ____

If you had known there was a law prohibiting psychiatrists from disclosing what patients tell them, would you have sought treatment earlier? . . . . Yes _____ No _____

On what did you most strongly rely to guarantee the privacy of your communication to the psychiatrist? (Rate: 1 for strongly, 2 for next most strongly, and 3 for least strongly):

a) His ethics? . . . . _________

b) The generally accepted principle that the doctor-patient relationship is confidential? . . . . _________

c) A law forbidding disclosure? . . . . _________

Have you ever wondered if there is a law prohibiting the psychiatrist from telling what you tell him? . . . . Yes _____ No _____

Have you ever asked if such a law exists? . . . . Yes _____ No _____

If you answered (8) YES and (9) NO, why not? _____________________________

____

Was there anything you withheld from your psychiatrist? . . . . Yes _____ No _____

What kinds of information did you withhold? (check all applicable)

a. Thoughts of violence?	_____	e. Financial issues?	_____
b. Acts of violence?	_____	f. Possible crimes?	_____
c. Sexual thoughts?	_____	g. Drugs or medications taken?	_____

d. Sexual acts? _____ h. Other (specify) _____

Would the existence of a law prohibiting a psychiatrist from disclosing what you tell him have encouraged you to be more open with him?. . . . . Yes _____ No _____

Age: ____ Sex: ____ Marital Status: S____ M____ W____ D____ Occupation: __________

Length of Time in Therapy: __________ Approximate Number of Sessions: __________

TABLE 3
THERAPIST PRIVILEGE QUESTIONNAIRE

Age ______ Sex ______ Years in Practice ______

County Population (check one)—

Less than 10,000 ____ 10–50,000 ____ 50–100,000 ____ 100,000+ ____

Type of practice (check one)

a. Full-time outpatient (private) ____
b. Full-time inpatient and outpatient (private) ____
c. Part-time private practice (20 hours/week or less) ____
d. Institutional practice ____

Approximate number of patients seen per week ____

Usual frequency of outpatient visits (sessions per patient per week) ____

Type of psychotherapy practiced (check all applicable)

a. Psychoanalysis ____
b. Psychoanalytic psychotherapy ____
c. Sex therapy ____
d. Marital counseling ____
e. Behavior therapy ____
f. Supportive psychotherapy ____
g. Hypnosis ____
h. Transactional analysis ____
i. Gestalt therapy ____
j. Cognitive therapy ____
k. Rational-Emotive therapy ____
l. Other(s) (specify) ______ ____

Have you ever been requested to disclose in court information revealed to you in therapy? Yes ____ No ____

a. How many times has this happened to you? ______
b. Were you forced to disclose at any time? Yes ____ No ____
c. If your answer to #5b is "No," for one or more cases, how did you avoid disclosure? (tell about each instance) ______

______

(use back of page if necessary)

If you did disclose, were any of your patients psychologically harmed by your disclosure? Yes ____ No ____

a. In what *psychological* way were they harmed (i.e., not loss of job or of child support, but of self-esteem or ability to cope) ______

______

How many of the patients about whom you disclosed were in therapy at the time of your disclosure? ______

a. Did any terminate prematurely because of the disclosure? Yes ______ No ______

b. Was therapy affected, and if so, in what way? Specify for each case if you can. ______

______

______

How many of the patients about whom you disclosed had terminated therapy with you? ______

a. Did any return to therapy afterward? Yes ______ No ______

b. If not, why not? ______

______

Have you ever warned a person who was *not* a professional directly involved with your patient's treatment that you thought your patient might harm him? (i.e., spouse, friend) Yes ______ No ______

a. How many times last year? ______

b. How many times in your career? ______

c. If your answer to #9 was "Yes," did it affect your therapy of your patient? ______

1) If "Yes," in what way? ______

______

2) If "Yes," did the patient terminate prematurely? Yes ______ No ______

Do you ever discuss patients with colleagues? Yes ______ No ______

a. If "Yes," what do you discuss about your patients? ______

______

Do you ever take the initiative in raising questions of confidentiality with your patients? Yes ______ No ______

a. If "Yes," under what circumstances? ______

______

b. Why? ______

______

What do you tell patients if they ask you if you will keep what they say in strict confidence?

______

a. How do your patients react? ______

______

Do you think that the present legal status of confidentiality in your state limits what some of your patients tell you? Yes ______ No ______

a. If so, why? ______

______

Do you think that there is a legal privilege protecting communications between a psychotherapist and his patient in your state? Yes ______ No ______

TABLE 4
JUDICIAL QUESTIONNAIRE

INSTRUCTIONS: Psychotherapist, as used below, is intended to include a psychiatrist, psychologist, physician, or other health care professional, treating a mental or emotional condition.

1. What is the population of the district in which your court is located:
   a. under 10,000 ______
   b. 10,000–50,000 ______
   c. 50,000–100,000 ______
   d. Over 100,000 ______
2. What percentage of cases you hear are:
   a. Domestic ______
   b. Criminal ______
   c. Mental Health ______
   d. Misc. Civil ______
3. How long have you been a judge of this court? ______ years
4. How many cases in your court have involved the admission of a statement made in confidence by a patient to his psychotherapist? (Approx. number) ______
5. When a question of admitting confidential communications between psychotherapist and patient arose in a case, were you of the opinion that the information involved was (check appropriate blank):

	Often	*Rarely*	*Never*
a. Important to the case.	____	____	____
b. Necessary for accurate resolution of contested factual issues.	____	____	____
c. Available from non-privileged sources.	____	____	____
d. Sought to encourage settlement.	____	____	____
e. Sought only to harass.	____	____	____
f. Other (specify).	____	____	____

6. When a confidential communication between a psychotherapist and patient is sought to be admitted, how do you resolve this issue:
   a. Always admit if relevant. ______
   b. Impose a higher standard of relevance. (If so, what?) ______
   c. Admit only if information not available from non-confidential source. ______
   d. Other (please specify). ______
7. Please describe briefly, any significant cases in which the admission of a confidential communication between patient and psychotherapist arose before you.

TABLE 5
DATA SUMMARY—LAY GROUPS
(n = 374)

	Texas		*West Va.*		*Quebec*		*Ontario*		*Totals*	
	n	%	*n*	%	*n*	%	*n*	%	*n*	%
Questionnaires:										
Distributed	200 (est.)		150 (est.)		97		100		550	
Returned	121	60.5%	103	69%	92	95%	58	58%	374	68%
Age:										
Range	17–57		18–63		19–64		18–60		17–64	
Median	24		20		24		23		23	
Mean	25.9		26.5		28.3		26		26.6	
Sex:										
Female	71	59%	46	47%	67	74%	41	71%	225	63%
Male	49	41%	42	43%	23	26%	17	29%	131	37%
Marital Status:										
Married	39	33%	27	27%	17	19%	6	10%	89	25%
Single	66	56%	63	64%	64	72%	45	78%	238	66%
Divorced	12	10%	8	8%	8	9%	7	12%	35	10%
Widowed	1	1%	0	0%	0	0%	0	0%	1	0%
Occupation:										
Office/Clerical	28	25%	8	9%	11	12%	5	9%	52	15%
Professional	13	12%	7	8%	11	12%	7	13%	38	11%
Student	11	10%	52	62%	53	60%	40	72%	156	46%
Sales	9	8%	3	4%	0	0%	0	0%	12	4%
Managerial	8	7%	0	0%	4	5%	1	2%	13	4%
Housewife	5	4%	1	1%	0	0%	0	0%	6	2%
Tech./Skilled Labor	24	22%	8	10%	6	7%	2	4%	40	12%
Unskilled Labor	12	11%	5	6%	1	1%	0	0%	18	5%
Other	0	0%	0	0%	3	3%	0	0%	3	1%

1. If you had a serious emotional problem, would you consider seeking help from a psychiatrist or psychologist?

Yes	112	92.5%	74	80%	74	80%	54	93%	314	86%
No	9	7.5%	19	2%	18	20%	4	7%	50	14%

2. If you would consider seeking such help and the following subjects were important, would you reveal them to the psychologist or psychiatrist?

	2. No cond.					7. No priv.				
	% Tx.	WVa.	Que.	Ont.	Avg.	% Tx.	WVa.	Que.	Ont.	Avg.
a. Speeding	86	94	70	86	(84)	49	53	40	46	(47)
b. Sexual fantasies	73	68	79	74	(74)	55	40	51	55	(50)
c. Physical violence	86	95	96	96	(92)	57	44	67	60	(57)

d. Masturbation	69	49	62	64	(61)	51	44	43	50	(47)
e. Work failure	89	97	92	93	(93)	48	55	46	53	(51)
f. Other sexual acts	74	73	58	79	(71)	54	44	47	50	(49)
g. Cheating on income tax	79	72	73	74	(75)	59	36	68	57	(55)
h. Theft	79	83	58	86	(77)	57	38	67	59	(55)
Average	79	79	74	81	(78)	53	57	54	54	(55)
Avg. Nondisc.	21	21	26	19	(22)	47	43	46	46	(44)

3. When you answered questions 1 and 2, did you consider that your psychologist or psychiatrist might be asked about your conversation with him?

a. By your insurance carrier	15	12%	20	21%	12	13%	2	3%	49	18%
b. By a state agency	17	14%	26	28%	15	16%	7	12%	65	24%
c. By a potential employer	18	15%	25	27%	17	18%	8	14%	68	25%
d. By a lawyer in a trial	27	22%	27	29%	21	23%	14	24%	89	33%

4. Is there a law in your state (province) that prevents a court from forcing a psychologist or psychiatrist called as a witness at a trial to state what his patient told him?

Yes	31	26%	20	19%	33	36%	26	45%	110	29%
No	9	7%	7	7%	7	7%	3	5%	26	7%
D/K	81	67%	76	74%	52	56%	29	50%	238	64%

5. If there is such a law, may the psychologist or psychiatrist be required to testify in any of the following situations?

a. You are charged with murder and what you told the psychologist and psychiatrist proves that you did it	73	60%	36	39%	52	57%	24	41%	185	51%
b. You sue someone for emotional injuries suffered in an accident, but the psychiatrist or psychologist thinks your problems started before the accident	48	40%	45	48%	55	60%	24	41%	172	48%
c. You and your spouse seek a divorce and fight over child custody and some										

things you told the psychologist or psychiatrist will not help your case	73	60%	33	36%	37	40%	13	22%	156	43%

6. Assume that the law in your state does prevent a court from forcing a psychologist or psychiatrist called as a witness at trial to state what his patient told him and the following subjects were important to your discussions with him or her. Would you reveal to the psychologist or the psychiatrist?

   (See answers to Question 2)

7. If there were no such law and a psychiatrist or psychologist could be forced to tell in court what you revealed in therapy, would it affect your discussion with the psychiatrist or psychologist of?

   (See answers to Question 2)

TABLE 6
DATA SUMMARY—PATIENT GROUPS

		Texas		*S.C./W.Va.*		*Quebec*		*Ontario*		*Totals*	
		n	%	*n*	%	*n*	%	*n*	%	*n*	%
Questionnaires:											
Mailed		155		95		200		200		650	
Returned		79	51%	41	43%	70	35%	64	32%	254	39%
Age:											
Range		17–59		19–65		20–72		23–69		17–72	
Median		36		33		37		36		35	
Sex:											
Female		57	73%	27	66%	39	62%	39	67%	162	68%
Male		21	27%	14	37%	24	38%	19	33%	78	32%
Marital Status:											
Married		42	53%	17	41%	27	43%	23	40%	109	46%
Single		22	28%	16	39%	21	33%	28	50%	87	37%
Divorced		12	18%	2	5%	14	22%	7	12%	35	15%
Widowed		1	1%	2	5%	1	2%	0	0%	4	3%
Occupation:											
Professional		22	31%	6	15%	24	40%	22	38%	74	32%
Housewife		10	14%	9	22%	2	3%	8	14%	29	13%
Office/Clerical		7	10%	6	17%	11	17%	7	12%	31	13%
Student		6	8%	10	24%	11	17%	6	10%	33	14%
Managerial		5	7%	2	5%	0	0%	5	9%	12	5%
Unskilled Labor		3	4%	0	0%	0	0%	0	0%	3	1%
Sales		2	3%	0	0%	2	3%	0	0%	4	2%
Tech/Skilled Labor		8	11%	0	0%	3	5%	5	9%	16	7%
Other		9	13%	7	17%	7	12%	5	12%	28	12%
Therapy:											
Range		1 wk–17 yrs.		1 wk–15 yrs.		3 wk–19 yrs.		3 wk–20 yrs.		1 wk–20 yrs.	
Median		3 years		8 months		2 years		2 years		2 years	
Median Frequency		Once a week		Once a week		Once a week		Once a week		Once a week	
1. Do you think there is a law which prohibits psychiatrists from disclosing what patients tell them to:											
(friends)	a. Yes	23	29%	24	62%	37	59%	27	47%	111	47%
	b. No	43	55%	12	30%	12	19%	19	33%	86	37%
	c. Don't know	12	15%	3	8%	13	21%	10	17%	38	16%
(colleagues)	a. Yes	13	17%	8	21%	23	37%	19	33%	63	27%
	b. No	50	65%	25	66%	26	41%	28	48%	129	55%
	c. Don't know	14	18%	5	13%	14	22%	10	17%	43	18%
(court)	a. Yes	21	27%	16	41%	25	40%	23	40%	85	36%

b. No	39	50%	16	41%	17	27%	23	40%	95	40%
c. Don't know	18	23%	7	18%	20	32%	12	20%	57	24%
2. Was the confidentiality of the doctor-patient relationship a consideration for you when you first started thinking about therapy?										
YES	43	54%	20	50%	39	62%	26	46%	128	54%
3. If your answer to (2) was "yes," was it:										
a. A very important consideration (you had great concern about the privacy of your communication)	16	20%	13	33%	17	44%	17	44%	63	32%
b. A not important consideration (you wondered briefly if your communication to the doctor might be disclosed, but didn't think further about it)	17	22%	5	13%	7	18%	7	18%	36	19%
c. Somewhere between (a) and (b)	10	13%	5	13%	15	38%	15	38%	45	23%
4. If you were concerned about the confidentiality of the relationship, did you ask the doctor about it?										
YES	22	28%	6	17%	20	32%	14	24%	62	26%
5. Did you take any steps to ensure the confidentiality of the relationship, like ask the doctor not to keep written records or obtain his word that he would not disclose what you told him?										
YES	10	13%	7	18%	9	14%	9	16%	35	15%
6. If you had known there was a law prohibiting psychiatrists from disclosing what patients tell them, would you have sought treatment earlier?										
YES	6	8%	4	11%	4	7%	0	0%	14	6%
7. On what did you most strongly rely to guarantee the privacy of your communication to the psychiatrist?										
a. His ethics	96%		86%		89%		94%		92%	
b. The generally accepted principle that the doctor-patient relationship is confidential	93%		100%		94%		90%		94%	

c. A law forbidding disclosure	12%		31%		38%		17%		19%	

8. Have you ever wondered if there is a law prohibiting the psychiatrist from telling what you tell him?

YES	35	45%	15	37%	22	35%	8	14%	57	33%

9. Have ever asked if such a law exists?

YES	8	10%	4	10%	8	13%	8	14%	28	12%

10. If you answered (8) "yes" and (9) "no," why not?

Relied on doctor's ethics or trust of the doctor	9		9		3		6		27	
Assumed/knew of such a law	3		10		2		5		20	
Not concerned	5		4		3		5		19	
No legal/criminal issue	3		3		1		0		7	
Wouldn't disclose if concerned about sharing					0		1		1	
Embarrassed	0		0		1		2		3	

11. Was there anything withheld from your psychiatrist?

YES	31	40%	19	46%	26	43%	19	33%	95	41%

12. What kind of information did you withhold?

a. Thoughts of violence	5	9%	5	12%	5	11%	8	17%	23	13%
b. Acts of violence	0	0%	0	0%	2	4%	3	6%	5	7%
c. Sexual thoughts	18	34%	10	25%	13	28%	16	34%	47	26%
d. Sexual acts	19	36%	9	23%	8	17%	8	17%	44	25%
e. Financial issues	5	9%	5	12%	8	17%	6	13%	24	13%
f. Possible crimes	2	4%	3	8%	1	2%	2	4%	8	5%
g. Drugs or medications taken	2	4%	3	8%	5	11%	3	6%	13	7%
h. Other	2	4%	6	14%	5	11%	1	2%	14	8%

13. Would the existence of a law prohibiting a psychiatrist from disclosing what you tell him have encouraged you to be more open with him?

Yes	Not asked		7	17%	6	10%	3	6%	16	10%

*Not all questionnaires received were tallied. Seven Quebec questionnaires and six Ontario questionnaires were lost.

TABLE 6A
PATIENT QUESTIONNAIRES COMPLETED BY STUDENTS IN THERAPY

Age: (n = 12)	Sex: (n = 12)	Marital Status: (n = 11)
Range = 23–61	F = 7 (58%)	M = 6 (55%)
Median = 31	M = 5 (42%)	D = 5 (45%)
	1:1	

Occupation: (n = 12)

Professional	4	33%
Office/Clerical	2	17%
Student	3	25%
Managerial	1	8%
Skilled technical	1	8%
Restaurant	1	8%

Therapy: Range = 1 week–13 years; Median = 3 months, most seen once a week

1. Do you think there is a law which prohibits psychiatrists from disclosing what patients tell them to: (n = 12)

a. the psychiatrist's friends:	Yes =	6	(50%)
	No =	6	(50%)
b. the psychiatrist's professional colleagues:	Yes =	1	(9%)
	No =	11	(91%)
c. a court of law:	Yes =	4	(33%)
	No =	8	(67%)

2. Was the confidentiality of the doctor-patient relationship a consideration for you when you first started thinking about therapy? (n = 12)
   Yes = 8 (67%)

3. If your answer to (2) was "yes," was it: (n = 7)

a. A *very* important consideration (you had great concern about the privacy of your communication)	4	(33%)
b. A *not* important consideration (you wondered briefly if your communication to the doctor might be disclosed, but didn't think further about it)	1	(8%)
c. Somewhere between (a) and (b)	2	(16%)

4. If you were concerned about the confidentiality of the relationship, did you ask the doctor about it? (n = 12)
   Yes = 6 (50%)

5. Did you take any steps to ensure the confidentiality of the relationship, like ask the doctor not to keep written records or obtain his word that he would not disclose what you told him? (n = 12)
   Yes = 3 (25%)

   a. What did you do?

Asked the doctor not to disclose	1
Asked if he kept notes	1
Closed door, turned off recorder	1

6. If you had known there was a law prohibiting psychiatrists from disclosing what patients tell them, would you have sought treatment earlier? (n = 12)

   Yes = 4 (33%)

7. On what did you most strongly rely to guarantee the privacy of your communication to the psychiatrist?

a. His ethics	75%
b. The generally accepted principle that the doctor-patient relationship is confidential	100%
c. A law forbidding disclosure	45%

8. Have you ever wondered if there is a law prohibiting the psychiatrist from telling what you tell him? (n = 12)

   Yes = 6 (50%)

9. Have you ever asked if such a law exists? (n = 12)

   Yes = 2 (16%)

10. If you answered (8) "yes" and (9) "no," why not?

Relied on doctor's ethics or trust of the doctor	3
Took for granted	1

11. Was there anything withheld from your psychiatrist? (n = 12)

    Yes = 6 (50%)

12. What kind of information did you withhold (n = 13 items withheld)

a. Thoughts of violence	1	(8%)
b. Acts of violence	1	(8%)
c. Sexual thoughts	4	(31%)
d. Sexual acts	2	(15%)
e. Financial issues	1	(8%)
f. Possible crimes	2	(15%)
g. Drugs or medications taken	1	(8%)
h. Other	1	(8%)

13. Would the existence of a law prohibiting a psychiatrist from disclosing what you tell him have encouraged you to be more open with him? (n = 11)

    Yes = 5 (45%)

TABLE 7
DATA SUMMARY—THERAPISTS

	Texas		*S.C./W.Va.*		*Quebec*		*Ontario*		*Totals*	
	n	%	*n*	%	*n*	%	*n*	%	*n*	%
Questionnaires:										
Mailed	186		248		427		445		1306	
Returned	84	48%	48	19%	107*	25%	81*	18%	320	25%
Respondents:										
Median age	44		42		47		45		45	
Mean age	45.2									
Median years in practice	11		11		16		13		13	
Average	13.8									
Male:female ratio	4:1		12:1		6:1		3.5:1		4.8:1	
1. Type of Practice										
Full-time outpatient (private)	28	33%	4	8%	17	20%	15	25%	64	23%
Full-time outpatient and inpatient (private)	27	32%	20	42%	20	24%	10	17%	77	28%
Part-time practice (less than 20 hours/week)	13	15%	5	10%	19	23%	13	22%	50	18%
Institutional practice	16	20%	19	40%	28	34%	23	38%	86	31%
2. Average number of patients seen per week										
	30		41		26		24		32	
3. Median frequency of outpatient visits per week										
	1		1		1		1		1	
4. Type of psychotherapy practiced (multiple responses permitted)										
Psychoanalytic psychotherapy	76	90%	28	58%	71	86%	38	63%	213	77%
Supportive psychotherapy	63	75%	44	92%	65	78%	36	60%	194	70%
Marital counseling	45	53%	29	60%	23	28%	25	42%	122	48%
Behavior therapy	15	18%	14	29%	20	24%	10	17%	59	22%
Psychoanalysis	13	15%	1	2%	22	27%	9	15%	45	16%
Cognitive therapy	12	14%	18	38%	19	23%	12	20%	61	22%
Hypnosis	11	13%	11	23%	4	5%	4	7%	30	11%
5. How many therapists had been requested to disclose in court information revealed in therapy?										
	39	48%	30	62%	29	35%	25	42%	123	45%
a. How many										

times—median	2		2		0		0		1	
b. How many of those requested to disclose were later forced to disclose?	13	15%	13	27%	6	7%	7	12%	39	14%
6. If the therapist did disclose, were patients psychologically harmed?										
YES†	0	0%	6	23%	9	30%	3	43%	18	29%
7. Of the therapists who disclosed about patients who were in therapy at the time—	23		20		24		14		81	
a. How many therapists reported that patients terminated prematurely because of the disclosure?	2	9%	3	15%	7	23%	4	22%	16	20%
b. Was therapy affected? YES	2	25%	6	13%	10	36%	4	22%	22	21%
8. Of the patients about whom therapists disclosed who had terminated therapy—	21 pts (approx) 15 respond.		46 pts (approx) 13 respond.		104 **pts 13 respond.		10 pts 9 respond.		181 (approx.)	
a. How many therapists had patients who returned to therapy afterward?	5	33%	9	69%	9	45%	4	44%	27	47%
9. How many therapists had warned an endangered third party—	40	48%	23	48%	16	20%	22	37%	101	37%
a. Average number of warnings last year	0.3		0.6		0.16		0.38		.29	
b. How many times in a career (median)	1		1		0		0		1	
c. Did it affect therapy? YES‡	16	42%	12	50%	15	94%	10	45%	53	53%
(1) Did patients terminate prematurely? YES‡	4	10%	8	35%	3	19%	10	45%	25	25%
10. How many therapists discuss patients with colleagues?	80	95%	43	91%	70	84%	52	96%	245	91%
11. What percent of therapists sometimes take the initiative in raising the issue of confidentiality?										

	67	85%	39	81%	56	68%	53	91%	215	80%
12. What do therapists tell patients if they ask if the therapist will keep what they say in strict confidence?										
Yes, unless self or others endangered	36	47%	13	27%	12	16%	15	27%	76	24%
Yes, unless ordered by court	27	35%	12	25%	8	11%	0	0%	47	24%
Yes, as far as law allows	0	0%	0	0%	10	13%	25	45%	35	11%
Yes, absolutely	9	12%	12	25%	39	51%	11	20%	71	22%
13. What percent of therapists think that the present status of confidentiality in their state/province limits of what their patients tell them?										
	16	22%	17	37%	18	22%	20	36%	71	28%
14. What percentage of therapists knew or guessed correctly the status of psychotherapists–patient privilege in their state/province?										
	35	45%	40	85%	44	54%	38	67%	157	60%

*The origin of 43 returned questionnaires could not be traced. Of these, 22 were assigned to Quebec and 21 to Ontario. These questionnaires were not tallied.

†One respondent reported 90 disclosures. Numbers refer to numbers of therapists who reported that patients were harmed.

‡Number of therapists, not number of patients

**One respondent indicated 90 disclosures

TABLE 8
DATA SUMMARY—JUDICIAL

	Texas		*S.C./W.Va.*		*Quebec*		*Ontario*		*Totals*	
	n	%	*n*	%	*n*	%	*n*	%	*n*	%
Questionnaires:										
Mailed	56		183		129		97		465	
Returned	48	86%	74	40%	38	29%	32	33%	192	41%
3. How long have you been a judge of this court?										
Range	1–8 years		0–31 years		1–20 years		1.5–23 years			
Median	3.5 years		6 years		7 years		9 years			
4. How many judges reported hearing cases involving admission of statements made in confidence to psychotherapist?	15	31%	33	45%	19	50%	9	28%	76	40%
5. When a question of admitting confidential psychotherapist-patient communications arose in a case, was the information:										
a. Important to the case	13	87%	20	61%	7	35%	7	70%	47	62%
b. Necessary for accurate resolution of contested factual issues	10	67%	19	58%	4	20%	5	50%	38	50%
c. Available from nonprivileged sources	2	13%	16	48%	10	50%	2	20%	30	39%
d. Sought to encourage settlement	0	0%	10	30%	2	10%	2	20%	14	18%
e. Sought only to harrass	1	7%	4	12%	2	10%	0	0%	7	9%
6. When a confidential communication between a psychotherapist and patient is sought to be admitted, how do you resolve this issue?										
a. Always admit if relevant	10	67%	25	76%	8*	40%*	5*	56%	48	62%
b. Impose higher standard of relevance	3	13%	3	9%	2	10%	3	33%	10	13%
c. Admit only if unavailable from nonconfidential sources	1	7%	9	27%	4	20%	5	56%	19	25%

*Only with patient's consent

TABLE 9
INSURANCE STUDY

	1976	*1977*	*1978*	*1979*	*1980*
Initial psychiatric interview	10,174	10,829	8,560	10,230	9,682
Psychotherapy, 1 hour	39,462	35,405	40,753	47,873	41,293
Psychotherapy, half hour	130,171	134,252	113,072	102,933	100,734
Psychotherapy, 45 minutes	–	4,789	6,853	9,023	18,581
Psychotherapy, group, 1½ hours	9,256	8,051	8,631	8,995	13,180
Total Sessions	189,063	193,326	177,869	179,054	183,470

Chapter 6

PRIVILEGE REVISITED

Common law courts[1] and evidence scholars[2] have structured their analysis of the rules of evidence to favor the receipt of probative evidence and to cast upon those who would exclude probative evidence the burden of persuasion that some rule or policy should justify its exclusion. In the case of the psychotherapist-patient privilege, proponents of the privilege have attempted to sustain this burden primarily through the utilitarian argument in favor of the privilege, arguing that, in its absence, effective psychotherapy would not be possible.[3] As the previously discussed research on the utilitarian argument indicates, the utilitarian proponents of a psychotherapist-patient privilege have not carried the day.[4] It is not at all clear from the available empirical research data that, in the absence of a psychotherapist-patient privilege, effective psychotherapy cannot or does not occur. For most people, the role of secrecy in the decision to enter therapy and the course of therapy turns on professional ethics and is unaffected by the existence of a privilege. According to traditional common law evidence scholarship, proponents of a privilege bear the burden of justifying the exclusion of probative evidence. Thus, whatever doubts remain about the consequences of a privilege on effective psychotherapy, more research is necessary to justify recognition of a psychotherapist-patient privilege on utilitarian grounds. Rejection of a psychotherapist-patient privilege based upon utilitarian grounds does not, however, require that the notion of a psychotherapist-patient privilege be rejected.

The deontological argument for a psychotherapist-patient privilege,[5] frequently ignored by the privilege's proponents in common law jurisdictions,[6] is persuasive both on its own terms and as a vehicle for avoiding the quagmire created by the assumptions underlying the utilitarian arguments. This deontological argument, which posits that regardless of its specific consequences to the psychotherapist-patient relationship, it is inappropriate for the government to intrude upon this private sphere of interpersonal communications, is compelling. In general, we recoil at the notion of the government intruding upon our private communications, not because we fear that husband-wife or parent-child relationships will break down, but because we think it inappropriate for the government to play this intrusive role in a democratic society. Our expectations of privacy include the notion that we are entitled to an inner sanctum immune from governmental intrusion. This is reflected in the Fourth Amendment of the United States Constitution and other more recent privacy legislation.[7] Because psychotherapist-patient communications regularly involve revelations from that inner sanctum, they seem specially worthy of protection.

Yet, even though we may as a society reject broad intrusions into these private communications, there is nonetheless a recognition even by deontological proponents of a psychotherapist-patient privilege that certain considerations may justify intrusion.[8] Even in civil law jurisdictions that recognize a medical privilege or professional secret based on a deontological rationale, the limitation on disclosure is not absolute. Other considerations may justify disclosure.[9] Agreement on these considerations, valued higher than relational privacy, is not likely to be uniform from jurisdiction to jurisdiction or commentator to commentator. Some might permit exceptions in cases of child abuse or child custody, others only in the case of national security.

In the case of a psychotherapist-patient privilege based on a utilitarian rationale, it is necessary to decide in advance of litigation the requirements for recognizing of the privilege and its exceptions. This is because the utilitarian argument for the privilege posits that people choose to enter into therapy or to make disclosures in therapy based on their knowledge of the applicable law. Thus a fixed, ascertainable rule and exceptions is a necessary response to a privilege based upon a utilitarian rationale. Once the utilitarian rationale is rejected and a deontological basis for the privilege is substituted, a different approach to the structure of the privilege and its exceptions is possible. No longer need it be assumed that the privilege and its exceptions must be fixed in advance of litigation so that people may choose to enter into therapy or make candid disclosures based upon it. Research on the assumptions underlying the utilitarian rationale reveal that most people do not rely on the privilege to decide whether to enter into therapy, make disclosures in therapy, or trust their therapist. Rather the privilege exists, according to the deontological rationale, because the value that is placed on this aspect of relational privacy is more important than other competing values. But, since it is recognized that some exceptions to the privilege should also exist in the case of the deontologically based privilege, a method of balancing these competing values, articulating, and applying these exceptions must be developed.

It is not particularly helpful to ask in the abstract whether the value of protecting confidentiality in the psychotherapist-patient relationship is more important, for example, than the correct adjudication of a child custody case. An intelligent response to this question involves a series of further questions: What is the nature of the psychotherapist-patient relationship involved in this case? Why do we need this evidence in the child custody case; what are the actual issues in the case; and, how would this evidence bear on these issues? Are other sources of evidence on these issues available that do not involve the use of a confidential source? What are the consequences of an erroneous decision in this case? Only as the facts of the given case develop can answers to these questions occur. Therefore, instead of fixing the ambit of the privilege prior to the onset of litigation as required by the utilitarian-based privilege, a balance of the competing values under a deontological rationale should be made at that point in the case when much of the evidence has been developed and the issues in the case made clearer.

Both opponents and proponents of the privilege may be alarmed at the prospect of vesting substantial discretion in trial court judges to decide whether a privilege ought to be allowed in a given case, not by applying a legislatively predetermined rule, but by a balancing of values. The caliber of the trial court judiciary, their values, and the absence of any talisman for correct answers are all legitimate concerns raised by this proposal. Yet this proposal is not as radical as it may sound initially.

The use of broad judicial discretion in balancing competing values as a vehicle for ascertaining the admission of evidence is not without precedent in our evidentiary system. For example, rule 609(d) of the Federal Rules of Evidence dealing with the admissibility of juvenile convictions provides that juvenile adjudications are not admissible under the general rule of Rule 609, however, this subsection creates an exception that ultimately involves balancing of values by the trial court judge:

> Evidence of juvenile adjudications is generally not admissible under this rule. The court may, however, in a criminal case allow evidence of the juvenile adjudication of the witness other than the accused if conviction of the offense would be admissible to attack the credibility

> of an adult and the *court is satisfied that admission in evidence is necessary for a fair trial determination of the issue of guilt or innocence.*[10]

A review of the cases decided under the authority of this subsection reveals careful case by case analysis of the arguments in favor of disclosure and the policy behind nondisclosure of juvenile convictions.[11] The decisions correspond to the facts of the particular case and in no event give rise to "floodgate" fears either in the direction of exclusion or admission of this evidence.

Other specific privilege statutes in fact provide as a boiler-plate exception that the trial judge may in the interest of justice demand the revelation of otherwise privileged communications. North Carolina's physician-patient privilege is an example of such a provision.

> No person, duly authorized to practice physic or surgery, shall be required to disclose any information which he may have acquired in attending a patient in a professional character, and which information was necessary to enable him to prescribe for such patient as a physician, or to do any act for him as a surgeon and no such information shall be considered public records under G.S. 132-1. Confidential information obtained in medical records shall be furnished only on the authorization of the patient, or if deceased, the executor, administrator, or, in the case of unadministered estates, the next of kin. Any resident or presiding judge in the district, either at the trial or prior thereto, or the Industrial Commission pursuant to law may, subject to G.S. 8-53.6, compel such disclosure, *if in his opinion the same is necessary to a proper administration of justice.*[12]

This exception vesting substantial discretion in the trial court to except the privilege has existed since at least 1885[13] and has been continued in amendments to the privilege for over 100 years without apparent problems. To require that each decision be made based upon maximum knowledge of the particular circumstances of each individual case, only the trial judge in that case may order disclosure under this provision.[14] The standards for disclosure have evolved to require a showing of need for the evidence in the given case and a cogent reason why the privilege's protection ought not to extend to these circumstances.[15] The decisions here, as well as those under Federal Rule of Evidence 609(d), correspond to the facts of each case and do not suggest abuses in the direction of exclusion or admission of this evidence.

More specifically, the Law Reform Commission of Canada proposed a general professional privilege whose application and exceptions would involve balancing by the trial judge.

> A person who has consulted a person exercising a profession for the purpose of obtaining professional services, or who has been rendered such services by a professional person, has a privilege against disclosure of any confidential communication reasonably made in the course of the relationship if, in the circumstances, the public interest and the privacy of the relationship outweighs the public interest and the administration of justice.[16]

Although this particular provision has not yet been enacted, in many ways it reflects the noncodified practice in common law Canada.[17] Even in the absence of a formal privilege for psychiatrist-patient communications, judges have used the discretion allotted them in assessing contempt citations to balance the confidentiality of the relationship with the significance of the case at hand and the importance of the confidential communication to it.

Some might criticize the balancing approach, arguing that the absence of a specific rule and specific exceptions does not permit certainty and predictability in application of the law. To respond to this criticism, it is appropriate first to point out the fact that studies of the utilitarian basis for the privilege question the extent to which people rely on knowledge of the applicable law to make decisions about commencement of therapy or disclosure within therapy. If the applicable law was consulted by prospective patients, they would discover in most jurisdictions a series of ambiguous exceptions to each privilege that would, as rational planners, leave them much less certain about the application of the privilege to a given situation than proponents of uniformity would care to admit.[18] Nonetheless, the data suggest that despite these varying rules, judges in different jurisdictions operate in much the same way with regard to compelled disclosure of confidential psychotherapist-patient communications.[19]

The feared absence of certainty or predictability of results with a balancing approach to privilege can be addressed by providing a methodology for trial judges in balancing these competing values. At the outset, because of the policy considerations favoring privacy, in the absence of other compelling considerations, the presumption should be in favor of preserving confidentiality of psychotherapist-patient relationships which meet certain requirements. These minimal requirements need not differ from the prerequisites now imposed for the recognition of a psychotherapist-patient privilege. An individual wanting treatment must seek out a licensed therapist. The communication at issue must be confidential and pertinent to treatment. Once these minimal requirements are found to exist, a presumption in favor of protecting the confidentiality of these communications should come into existence.

To rebut this presumption the trial judge should be asked to consider a number of factors. First, what are the competing values at stake? As against the value of privacy, what is the potential benefit to be gained by disclosure in this given case? Thus, for example, in terms of the benefit to be gained by disclosure ascertaining damages correctly in an automobile collision case would seem less important to society than the correct adjudication of a custody case involving a very young child.

Next, the trial judge should consider the importance of the evidence in this case. If the trial judge had this particular piece of evidence, would it likely play a substantial role in his decision? If, for example, in a child custody case, the evidence sought to be adduced through the psychotherapist consisted of a disclosure in therapy of an extramarital affair conducted after the parties separated and not conducted in the presence of the children, the trial judge might reasonably conclude that although this evidence would meet a minimal relevance threshold, it is not sufficiently important in deciding custody to justify compelled disclosure. If, on the other hand, the father encouraged the children to watch him have sexual relations with his woman friend, this ought to be construed as highly relevant. The argument that such decisions would call for great technical expertise on the part of judges can be countered by the observation that most decisions of this sort require only common sense.

Finally, the trial judge should consider alternative sources of evidence. Has the attorney demonstrated an attempt to obtain this evidence elsewhere or is this simple laziness? Is the evidence redundant? Have other witnesses testified from non-privileged sources to the same event? Is the event to which the testimony is addressed contested? If the same or equivalent evidence has been presented or could be if the proponent was diligent or if the issue is not contested, disclosure should not be compelled.

The later in the litigation these questions of importance and alternatives arise, the better informed the trial judge will be in making these decisions. In many instances, however, the parties will desire a ruling on these questions during discovery to prepare for trial. Although the scope of discovery is generally broader than the rules of evidence governing admissibility at trials, the privilege rules remain the same.[20] Thus, the issue may come to a head at this earlier time.

Two approaches may lessen this problem. One is to erect a standing protective order regularly scheduling discovery on these issues at the end of the discovery process. The other related approach is to examine critically the information previously obtained through discovery to ascertain whether it yields alternate sources of the same information or suggests its potential importance at trial.

Often, in federal court, a magistrate and not the district court judge assigned the case will hear discovery motions. In many state courts discovery motions will also not be heard by the judge assigned the case. Because of the constitutional magnitude of the application of the psychotherapist-patient privilege and the degree of discretion involved in this approach, the lessons learned in North Carolina should not be forgotten. Only the trial judge assigned the case should be permitted to rule on the applicability of the psychotherapist-patient privilege.

This overall, more flexible approach is designed to yield a more exacting accommodation of competing values. It values relational privacy, but recognizes that where the issue is in fact extremely important in the litigation and the litigation involves important stakes and good lawyering has not yielded other sources of the same information, it may be disclosed. As with any response involving discretion it raises the possibility of an abuse of discretion. Yet the alternative yields an inexact response to the competing values and ignores the realities of existing judicial practice.

FOOTNOTES, CHAPTER 6

1. Testimonial exclusionary rules and privileges contravene the fundamental principle that "the public . . . has a right to every man's evidence." United States v. Bryan, 339 U.S. 323, 331 (1950). As such, they must be strictly construed and accepted "only to the very limited extent that permitting a refusal to testify or excluding relevant evidence has a public good transcending the normally predominant principle of utilizing all rational means for ascertaining truth." Elkins v. United States, 364 U.S. 206, 234 (1960) (Frankfurter, J., dissenting). Accord, United States v. Nixon, 418 U.S. 683, 709–10 (1974).

   Trammel v. United States, 445 U.S. 40, 50–51 (1980).
2. 8 J. Wigmore, A Treatise on the Anglo American System of Evidence in Trials at Common Law § 2285 (McNaughten rev. ed. 1961); McCormick, *The Scope of Privilege in the Law of Evidence,* 16 Tex. L. Rev. 447 (1938).

3. E.g., Guttmacher & Weihofen, *Privileged Communications Between Psychiatrist and Patient,* 28 Ind. L.J. 32 (1952); Slovenko, *Psychiatry and a Second Look at the Medical Privilege,* 6 Wayne L. Rev. 175 (1960); Group for the Advancement of Psychiatry. Report No. 45, Confidentiality and Privileged Communication in the Practice of Psychiatry (Report No. 45, 1960).
4. See Chapter 5.
5. Krattenmaker, *Testimonial Privileges in Federal Courts—Alternative to the Proposed Federal Rules of Evidence,* 62 Geo. L.J. 61 (1973); Louisell, *Confidentiality, Conformity and Confusion: Privileges in Federal Court Today,* 31 Tul. L. Rev. 101 (1957).
6. The psychotherapist-patient privilege proposed in the Federal Rules of Evidence [Proposed Fed. R. Evid. 504], the California Evidence Code [Cal. Evid. Code §§ 1010–1026 (West Supp. 1981)], and the Connecticut Evidence Code [Conn. Gen. Stat. Ann. § 52-146(c) (West Supp. 1981)], the most significant proposals for codification with legislative histories, all relied exclusively upon utilitarian justifications. The rationale for the civil law counterpart to privilege, professional secret, relies extensively on a deontological rationale for recognition of a medical secret limiting disclosure of relational communications. See Chapter 4.
7. Privacy Protection Act of 1980, 42 U.S.C. §§ 2000aa et seq.
8. Saltzburg, *Privileges and Professionals: Lawyer and Psychiatrists,* 66 Va. L. Rev. 597. 602 (1980).
9. See Chapter 4.
10. Fed: R. Evid. 609(d) (emphasis added).
11. *See, e.g.,* Leonard v. Argento, 699 F.2d 874, 894–96 (7th Cir. 1983), cert. denied 104 S. Ct. 69 (1983) (admissibility of plaintiff's 24 year old juvenile conviction in civil rights action following arrest at scene of automobile accident too remote and unrelated to truth telling to justify admission); United States v. Nogueira, 585 F.2d 23, 25 (1st Cir. 1978) (inquiry into chief prosecution witness's juvenile adjudication for attempted car larceny permitted in bank robbery prosecution); United States v. Lind, 542 F.2d 599 (2nd Cir. 1976) (limited inquiry into facts underlying victim's juvenile conviction for hitchhiking permitted in prosecution for kidnapping).
12. N.C. Gen. Stat. § 8-53 (Supp. 1981) (emphasis added). To the same effect is section 49 of Israel's Evidence Ordinance that provides that medical privilege does not apply when the "Court has found that the necessity to disclose the evidence for the purpose of doing justice outweighs the interest in its non-disclosure."
13. Ch. 159, Laws of N.C., 1885; Sims v. Charlotte Liberty Mutual Ins. Co. 256 N.C. 32, 125 S.W.2d 326, 329 (1962).
14. Lockwood v. McCaskill, 261 N.C. 754, 136 S.E.2d 67 (1964); Carter v. Colonial Life and Accid. Ins. Co., 278 S.E.2d 893 (N.C. App. 1981).
15. In re Albemarle Mental Health Center, 42 N.C. App. 292, 256 S.E.2d 818 (1979), cert. denied, 298 N.C. 297, 259 S.E.2d 298 (1979) (in camera hearing appropriate to determine whether potential information was relevant to homicide, and constituted privilege information and disclosure necessary in the interests of justice); Creech v. Sovereign Camp of the Woodman of the World, 211 N.C. 658,

191 S.E. 840 (1937) (attempt to show misrepresentation in insurance policy through deceased personal physician denied as not material to death caused by an unrelated condition).

16. Law Reform Commission of Canada, Evidence Code § 41.
17. Dickens, *Legal Protection of Psychiatric Confidentiality,* 1 Int. J. L. & Psychiatry 2455 (1978).
18. Texas, for example, has a psychotherapist-patient privilege. (Tex. R. Evid. 510.) However it is not applicable in criminal cases (Tex. Cr. R. Evid. 509), when it is relied on for a claim or defense (Tex. R. Evid. 510(d)(5)), or when it is relevant to the parent-child relationship (Tex. R. Evid. 510 (d)(6)). California's psychotherapist-patient privilege is followed by several pages of exceptions. Cal. Evid. Code §§ 1010–1026 (West 1986 and Crim. Supp. 1986). It is not reasonable to expect the lay populace to be aware or to be able to interpret these statutes.
19. See Chapter 5.
20. *See, e.g.,* Fed. R. Civ. P. 26(b)(1).

Chapter 7

REFLECTIONS ON THE USES AND LIMITATIONS OF EMPIRICAL RESEARCH IN THE LAW

I. The Utility of Empirical Research

Societal policy choices, like the decision to recognize a psychotherapist-patient privilege, are often posed in terms that require a factual conclusion about the past or future effect of a particular course of action. In the case of the utilitarian arguments for a psychotherapist-patient privilege, the decision is posed in terms that ask whether psychotherapy has been or will be less effective in the absence of a privilege. In other contexts, factual questions may also underlie the response to the framing of societal policy decisions. Have mandatory medical malpractice screening panels reduced the filing of frivolous medical malpractice actions? Will deregulation of the airline industry result in reduced prices to consumers? Common sense dictates that where available empirical studies of questions framed in this fashion exist or can be conducted, this information should be gathered to reduce the uncertainty surrounding these decisions. Anecdotal evidence or old wives' tales ought not to substitute for well designed empirical research in the resolution of factual uncertainty surrounding societal policy decisions.

Of course, conducting this research may not always be feasible. The cost of conducting the research may outweigh the importance of the information it may generate. The time required to conduct the research may exceed the time within which the societal decisions must be made. Or, the design of the research may pose serious ethical problems that cannot be resolved.

Even when these logistical or ethical problems are not present, existing legal doctrines often provide a disincentive to utilize relevant empirical research in social policy decisions.[1] The test for constitutionality of legislation not involving fundamental interests or suspect classifications, an inquiry into the rational nexus between legitimate legislative means and goals,[2] most often results in a cursory scrutiny. This test sends a signal to the legislature that the judiciary is largely unconcerned with the legislature's attempts to garner facts to support its decision. The message sent is that these are political decisions that should be corrected by the electorate and not the judiciary.

When judges engage in judicial notice of legislative facts, the facts upon which judicial lawmaking turns,[3] another disincentive to the garnering of the available empirical research exists. As contrasted with judicial notice of adjudicative facts, the who did what to whom in this case, no requirement exists to give notice to the parties and permit them an opportunity to be heard on this issue.[4] Thus, a judge may base a decision on a legislative fact first discovered by the parties when reviewing the judgment.

Some reasons for optimism do exist, however. From time to time, the Supreme Court has demonstrated a willingness to engage in more demanding scrutiny of the empirical basis for decisions.[5] And, a new generation of materials in law and social science provides a vehicle for increasing the sophistication of the next generation of lawyers in the techniques of social science research and its treatment by courts and legislatures.[6]

II. The Limits of Empirical Research

Having touted the benefits of empirical research, a caveat is in order. Empirical research is not a panacea for societal policy problems. Numbers crunched in computers may look impressive. But not all research is well designed or conducted and not all conclusions drawn from good research are valid. Correlation does not prove cause and effect. And, the risks of resting constitutional doctrines on empirical conclusions have been amply demonstrated.

Brown v. Board of Education,[7] the Supreme Court's decision holding segregated educational facilities unconstitutional relied, in part, upon research conducted by Professor Kenneth Clark and others that concluded that segregation thwarted the intellectual development of black school children, rather than the moral conclusion that segregation is wrong regardless of its effects. As the psychological validity of the conclusions about segregation and intellectual development came to be questioned in the years following *Brown*, the decision became vulnerable to attack on these grounds.[8]

Although the exclusionary rule, prescribing the exclusion of evidence obtained in violation of constitutional limitations, did not begin with a deterrence rationale,[9] in the 1960s this rational became the converted basis for the rule. The purpose of the exclusionary rule became the prevention of future constitutional violations by deterring law enforcement from seizing evidence that would not be admitted at trial.[10] After this change, research into the deterrent effect of the rule was conducted and has yet to yield convincing conclusions about the rule's deterrent effect.[11] The focus of the debate about the rationale for the rule has now shifted from deterrence.[12]

Other issues have presented similar problems of uncertainty following the conduct of empirical research. For example, studies examining the deterrent effect of capital punishment[13] and the difference in deliberations of 12 versus 6 person juries[14] have become mired in methodological debates that reveal little factual certainty.

Even when empirical research is well designed and conducted, the questions to which it may provide answers are limited. Putting aside any methodological challenges to the author's empirical studies of privilege, they reveal only the extent to which people rely on privilege in making therapeutic decisions. If privilege is therapeutically important, the question remains whether there are greater societal interests that militate against recognition of a privilege in particular situations. This decision is one involving a choice between competing values resolvable in a political or moral context not a scientific context. If privilege is therapeutically unimportant, the question remains whether there are other reasons to recognize a privilege on alternate grounds. Again, this decision involves a value choice rather than a cause and effect measure of human behavior. Scientific research may clarify this issue, it cannot resolve it.

The critical issue then is not simply whether more empirical research ought to be conducted, but when and how this research ought to be used. Before framing societal policy questions in terms that raise empirical questions, the availability of existing research or the feasibility of conducting new research ought to be examined. Concomitantly, the alternative of casting the question in a fashion that does not raise empirical questions ought be examined. When existing research or the feasibility of new research is problematic, the importance of examining the alternative of rephrasing the question in nonempirical terms increases.

FOOTNOTES, CHAPTER 7

1. Shuman, *Decisionmaking Under Conditions of Uncertainty*, 67 Judicature 326 (1984).
2. Williamson v. Lee Optical Co., 348 U.S. 483 (1955).
3. Davis, *An Approach to Problems of Evidence in the Administrative Process*, 55 Harv. L. Rev. 364, 402–416 (1942).
4. Fed. R. Evid. 201(a).
5. Griggs v. Duke Power, 401 U.S. 424 (1971); Craig v. Boren, 429 U.S. 190, 217 (1976) (Rehnquist, J. dissenting).
6. J. Monahan and L. Walker: Social Science in Law: Cases and Materials (1985); L. Friedman and S. Macaulay, Law and the Behavioral Sciences (2nd ed. 1976).
7. 347 U.S. 483 (1954).
8. Rosen, *History and State of the Art of Applied Social Research in the Courts*, in The Use/Nonuse/Misuse of Applied Social Research in the Courts (Saks and Baron eds. 1980); Cahn, *Jurisprudence*, 30 N.Y.U.L. Rev. 150 (1955; Van den Haag, *Social Science Testimony in the Desegregation Cases: A Reply to Professor Kenneth Clark*, 6 Vill. L. Rev. 69 (1960).
9. Weeks v. United States, 232 US 383 (1914).
10. Elkins v. United States, 364 U.S. 206, 217 (1960).
11. *See e.g.*, Nagel, *Testing the Effects of Excluding Illegally Seized Evidence*, 1965 Wisc. L. Rev. 283; Oaks, *Studying the Exclusionary Rule in Search and Seizure*, 37 U.Chi. L. Rev. 665 (1970).
12. See Kamisar, *Is the Exclusionary Rule "Illogical" or "Unatural" Interpretation of the Fourth Amendment*, 62 Judicature 66 (1978–79); Wilkey, *The Exclusionary Rule: Why Supress Valid Evidence?* 62 Judicature 214 (1978–79); Wingo, *Rewriting Mapp and Miranda: A Preference for Due Process*, 31 U. Kan. L. Rev. 219 (1983).
13. *See e.g.*, F. Sellin, *The Penalty of Death*, (1980); Ehrlich, *The Deterrent Effect of Capital Punishment: A Question of Life and Death*, 65 Am. Econ. Rev. 397 (1975).
14. *See e.g.*, Wiehl, *The Six Man Jury*, 4 Gonzaga L. Rev. 35 (1968); Zeisel and Diamond, *"Convincing Empirical Evidence" on the Six-member Jury*, 41 U. Chi. L. Rev. 281 (1974).

INDEX

W 740 S562p 1987
Shuman, Daniel W.
The psychotherapist-patient privilege.